CAREERS IN
THE HO...
INDUSTRY

SOLD
BY
DURHAM COUNTY COUNCIL

CAREERS IN THE HOLIDAY INDUSTRY
Carole Chester

Second Edition

Copyright © Kogan Page Limited 1985, 1989

All rights reserved. No reproduction, copy or transmission
of this publication may be made without written permission.

No paragraph of this publication may be reproduced, copied
or transmitted save with written permission or in accordance
with the provisions of the Copyright Act 1956 (as amended),
or under the terms of any licence permitting limited copying
issued by the Copyright Licensing Agency, 7 Ridgmount Street,
London WC1E 7AE.

Any person who does any unauthorised act in relation to
this publication may be liable to criminal prosecution and
civil claims for damages.

First published in Great Britain in 1985 by
Kogan Page Limited, 120 Pentonville Road,
London N1 9JN.
Second edition 1989.

British Library Cataloguing in Publication Data

Chester, Carole
   Careers in the holiday industry. - 2nd ed.
   (Kogan Page careers series).
   1. Great Britain. Tourist industries. -
   Careers guides
   I. Title
   338.4'79141'0023

ISBN 1-85091-720-5

Typeset by DP Photosetting, Aylesbury, Bucks
Printed and bound in Great Britain by
Richard Clay, The Chaucer Press, Bungay

Contents

Introduction   7
Are You Suited to Travel? 7; What Skills? 8; What Courses? 8; What Qualifications? 9; What Salaries? 9

Part 1

1. **Tour Operators**   17
   What is a Tour Operator? 17; How does a Tour Operation Work? 17; Career Possibilities 18; Freelance? 18; Becoming a Tour Operator 18; Is Tour Operation Work for You? 21; The Giant Tour Operators 24; The Self Catering Tour Operator 26; Courier/Resort Rep 28; Courses 28; Grants 30

2. **Travel Agencies**   31
   What is a Travel Agent? 31; Travel Agent Skills 32; Where Can You Go? 32; Qualifications 34; Courses 34

3. **Hotels**   39
   What Qualifications are Needed? 39; Picking the Right Area 40; The Chef 40; The Waiter/Waitress 41; The Receptionist 42; The Housekeeper 43; The Manager 44; Sales and Marketing 46; Hotel Group Reservations 47; Hotel Representation 47

4. **Airlines**   49
   Administration 49; Operations 49; The Steward/Stewardess 50; Reservations and Ticketing 51; Ground Staff 51; Working at Airports 52

5. **Tourist Offices**   54
   What is a Tourist Office? 54; Career Opportunities 54; The British Tourist Authority 55; National

Tourist Boards 55; The English Tourist Board 55; Regional Tourist Boards 55; Tourist Information Centres 56; Other Opportunities 56; The Tourist Guide 57; The Tour Manager 57

6. **Cruise Lines**   58
   Career Opportunities 58; The Steward 58; Kitchen Staff 59; The Purser 60; Deck and Engineer Officers 60; Radio Officers 61; Electrical Officers 61; Other Possibilities 61

7. **Other UK Holiday Operations**   62
   Boating Holidays 62; Holiday Centres 63; Health Clubs 64; Stately Homes 64; Bed and Breakfast 65; Country House Hotels 65; Coaching Companies 65; Rail Travel 66

8. **Business Travel**   68
   What is Business Travel? 68; Conference Travel 68; Incentive Travel 69

9. **Public Relations, Press and Promotion Work**   71
   The Travel PRO 71; The Travel Writer 72; The Travel Photographer 73

Part 2

10. **Courses and Training**   78
    Diploma and Certificate Courses 78; Degrees of the Council for National Academic Awards 90; University Degree Courses 91; ABTA-Approved Training Centres for YTS Courses 92

11. **Useful Addresses**   93
    Regional Advisory Councils 94

12. **Useful Publications**   95

Introduction

What does travel mean to you? The chance to see the wonders of the world? The opportunity of sampling five-star hospitality? The magic of the high seas or the excitement of breaking new destination barriers?

Who doesn't dream of sun-kissed islands and an unending flow of rum punches. In fact, who can't wait for holiday time to roll around again? But travel is more than lying in the sun or boarding Concorde - it's an Industry with a capital I. Our increasing technical knowledge, creating time-saving devices, has also created more leisure time. And travel - if only for a weekend away in the country - is what many people use their leisure time for. Tourism is good for the economy and employment and that's where you come in.

Let's not forget, though, the business side of travel, although it is only indirectly related to the holiday industry. Thanks again to modern forms of transport, the world has shrunk. Paris for lunch and Rome for dinner is no pipe dream but just another working day for some. Company executives do not need to rely on letters to communicate with counterparts abroad. The conference and incentive market is the fastest growing travel area of the 1980s.

Are You Suited to Travel?

There are so many aspects to travel that almost anyone can be suited to a career in this field. It is more a question of being able to pick your way through the myriad choices. Those with creative flair might look to marketing, promotion, public relations, journalism or photography; whereas those who can enthuse about someone else's idea or product may find their *métier* is sales. Individuals who prefer detailed organisational work, will find that a grounding in finance or computers will stand them in good stead. But, if your skills are in dealing with people, the service sector is a possibility.

Just think – an airline pilot or stewardess working in the travel industry, and a hairdresser or waiter on board a passenger liner, are both considered to be in travel-related professions. These days, hotel managers often shift from hotel to hotel around the world and chefs as famous as Anton Mosimann are constantly lecturing and visiting abroad.

What Skills?

It would be far too difficult to say you need a specific skill to obtain a specific job in travel. A lot of training is given once you have been employed. On the other hand, you could hardly expect to become a chef if you cannot boil an egg; nor a rep or courier if you hate the sight of people. If you thought serving others was beneath you, a ship's steward or cabin crew position is not for you.

Assess your own skills before you choose a career. Talk to your college careers office, your family and friends. Pay attention to your own presentation, be it the letters you write or your appearance. Be prepared to take a lowly post initially and work your way up from within. The best degree in the world is not going to make you a manager overnight.

What Courses?

What courses are best for you depends primarily upon which aspect of travel you intend to tackle. To help simplify matters, think of the tourism industry as three major sectors: accommodation and catering; travel and transport; and leisure, recreation and entertainment.

The greatest number of job opportunities lie in the first of these sectors. Courses to consider would therefore concentrate on hotel and catering management; sales and marketing; and administration, business and accounting skills. Management and marketing qualifications would also be useful in the recreational or leisure areas and the travel and transport fields; though the latter is not expanding quite so fast. There are limited opportunities with local authorities and government agencies in the tourism area, but applicants will be expected to be thoroughly knowledgeable about the product or area they are to promote, for anything but the most junior positions. Travel and tourism as a degree course subject is relatively new, so only a few courses are available. They are increasing yearly, however, and do cover business subjects within the tourism context. The current Minister for Tourism, John Lee, tells us that the annual turnover from tourism is £18 billion which creates 1.4 million jobs, growing at around 1,000 new jobs per week.

There are several important courses which you should consider as an A level student, or even as a 16-year-old school-leaver:

1. *BTEC* (Business and Technician Education Council) and *SCOTVEC* (Scottish Vocational Education Council) courses include hands-on work experience and last from two to four years, depending on whether you opt for full-time, sandwich or day-release training.
2. *HND* (Higher National Diplomas) in Business Studies are offered with travel and tourism options, by some 15 colleges.
3. *CPVE* (the Certificate of Pre-vocational Education) is sometimes a 6th-form option in schools or can be taken at a college of further education. It guarantees at least a few weeks' work experience during the year – your chance to prove to yourself and your employer that you're an asset to the tourism industry.
4. *CGLI* (City and Guilds of London Institute) feature practical training courses in all sectors of the industry, most lasting a year. Of particular interest are courses which lead to COTAC (Certificate of Travel Agency Competency); COTOP (Certificate of Tour Operations Practice); and COTICC (Certificate of Tourist Information Centre Competence).
5. *YTS* (Youth Training Scheme) is a two-year programme for 16-year-olds (one year for 17-year-olds in some cases); with several travel and catering-related schemes.

Note also that the ABTA National Training Board organises training for young people intent on work in the travel business, and that the Hotel and Catering Training Board offers similar assistance for work in the hotel and restaurant world.

What Qualifications?

Your qualifications are the certificates or diplomas acquired at the end of any of the afore mentioned (or other) courses. In a way, school exam passes are less important if you're prepared to study hard and start at the bottom. You don't necessarily need

GCE/GCSE passes to take the more basic training courses, though it is only fair to say that the higher your grades, the easier it is to skip those basics and start off at a further training level.

What Salaries?

Anything from £5,000 pa to £50,000 pa can be offered, according to the job. To give you some idea, the following ads were taken from 1988 trade publications.

LARGE AIRLINE COMPANY TICKET OFFICER

Due to internal promotion, this vacancy has arisen at our newly refurbished Regent Street ticket office. The post-holder will assist the supervisor in co-ordinating the smooth running of the office and ensuring our high service standards are met. He/she will also deputise for the supervisor as and when necessary. A minimum of 3 years' experience in fares and ticketing plus a thorough knowledge of computerised systems is required, as well as excellent interpersonnel and communication skills. Candidates should be able to demonstrate drive, enthusiasm and the ability to cope with pressure. In return, we offer a starting salary between £12,500–£13,400 depending on experience (including LWA plus 13 months) and excellent staff travel benefits. For further information and an application form please write or telephone.

COME AND JOIN US ...

We are one of the country's leading direct sell holiday companies. We now need more sales and telephone staff to join our friendly office in SW1. If you are sales-orientated, possess an excellent telephone manner, enthusiasm and bags of personality, join us in the reservations department.

We offer a good salary (c £7,000) to the right people, plus holiday concessions. Interested? Please apply with a brief CV.

BRISTOL £8,000 +
IN-HOUSE RESERVATIONIST
MAJOR HOTEL BOOKING COMPANY

Applications are invited from candidates with good communications skills, an excellent telephone manner and preferably experience in hotel reservations. Working within a busy travel department of a major international company, you will be responsible for receiving and placing hotel and conference bookings. Essential qualities required are self-motivation, tact and the ability to work under pressure. Excellent in-house training and incentive schemes available.

Please reply with CV.

DARTFORD BOROUGH COUNCIL

TOURISM DEVELOPMENT OFFICER
(POST NO. 1009)

£11,679–£12,432 incl (pay award pending)

This post within the Borough Council's Economic Development Unit involves a wide range of activities including: marketing and sales development work; and liaison with local and national travel agents, tour operators, hotels, carriers and handling organisations in both the UK and overseas. The post-holder will have sound marketing and sales experience and a good practical knowledge of the travel trade. We are looking for someone who can adopt a commercial approach in initiating and translating creative concepts into reality, and in developing joint promotions with the tourism industry.

The successful person will also be expected to organise and/or attend trade exhibitions, workshops, roadshows at home and abroad, and to generally assist with the day-to-day involvement of the economic development activities of the Borough Council.

A formal qualification or proven experience in marketing or in a related subject gained in the tourism or leisure field, is essential. Ability to communicate in a foreign language is desirable. A current, full driving licence is essential.

Please request further details and an application form in writing.

A number of vacancies have arisen within this large travel organisation.

BRISTOL

Branch Manager
c £10,000

SLOUGH, ADDLESTONE, RUGBY, LEIGHTON BUZZARD, BASILDON

Senior/Travel Consultants
£5,028–£7,105
Salary according to age and experience

FLIGHT DESK
Situated in Blackfriars

Long Haul Flight Consultant
Salary negotiable

Applications to:

NORTHWOOD

Branch Manager
c £12,000

Senior/Travel Consultants
£5,028–£7,105
Salary according to age and experience

Applications in writing to:

We welcome applications from suitably qualified people regardless of sex, marital status, race or disability.

Part 1

Chapter 1
Tour Operators

What is a Tour Operator?

A tour operator is anyone who has put together a holiday package to offer for sale. In most cases this means a company which has established respect and credibility. The company may be an independent one, one of a group of companies or a giant holiday operation like Thomson Holidays.

Travel agencies may also be tour operators if they create their own specialised holiday programmes, or they can be an affiliated retail element, eg, Thomas Cook. Usually though, they are straightforward retail outlets selling airline tickets and the packages of a number of operators in return for commission.

Most tour operators choose to sell their product through travel agencies because it gives them a wider coverage of the market, ie, throughout the country, but some sell direct to the public with the aid of publicity and advertising. The larger companies will offer a broad range of holidays; the smaller tend to specialise in a particular destination, age group or type of vacation such as skiing.

How does a Tour Operation Work?

The aim is to offer the customer something he/she could not obtain him/herself - at least without inconvenience, effort and, more than likely, greater expenditure. By purchasing airline seat space or hotel room accommodation in bulk, the operator is given a better price than the individual and is able to pass on some of that saving. Similarly, since the operator is involved in group movements, he/she can arrange airport transfers and inexpensive insurance easily.

Costing is one of the most important features: the wholesale price of every holiday segment must be added together, plus a built-in profit. Obviously, commission payments, operation costs and overheads must be taken into consideration before a final consumer price is reached, yet that final price must appeal to the customer if the package is to sell.

Career Possibilities

The giants have many divisions of work so the choice of careers in travel and tourism is a wide one. A firm like Thomson's will have its own accountancy department, personnel office and sales reps, for example. There are contracts managers and operations managers for different areas of the world, and couriers and reps in various destinations. A company as well known as this one will have a large management and marketing team plus its own press office and, not surprisingly, a big reservations staff.

Smaller companies operate likewise but with fewer staff and work titles that may encompass more than one area of the business. And that goes for the specialists, too, although knowledge of a specific language, sport, etc, will help you get to the top more quickly.

As far as the salary is concerned, for the person who builds his/her own tour operation, the sky's the limit. If you become the managing director of your own private company, you will be able to set your salary according to profits – or sell out to (or merge with) a larger holding company. Salaries in other mentioned areas are in line with those in other industries, though travel couriers are in a bracket to themselves.

Freelance?

No way! Not as a tour operator. But many reps and couriers are semi-freelance since they work on a seasonal basis as part-time employees, instead of full-time staff. Tour operators also need to show their product; hence a brochure must be compiled, written, illustrated and printed. This often requires freelance copywriters and travel photographers.

Becoming a Tour Operator

There are no set rules as to how to become a tour operator (as opposed to working for one). You cannot expect to become one overnight – indeed, it is generally accepted that you need a good few years in the travel industry before you could consider it – and yet an entrepreneurial person with a good idea can start a business that may eventually prove successful.

Case Studies

Churchill Family Holidays was started by two men in 1981, each with a vast amount of varied experience. Mike's background was almost all travel (a lot with Thomson's), starting as an overseas courier, moving into contracting and then back in the UK in the planning division and finally into sales. Between times, he worked in several travel agencies in a number of capacities. His partner Peter trained in marketing and finance although originally he took a degree in civil engineering.

It took them a year to obtain City financing which they acquired by showing there was a market for their product, and that they were offering something new and different; therefore, there was no competition.

> The hole in the market was that no tour operator was catering *exclusively* for families. Selling a family holiday is like selling two types of holiday simultaneously – pleasing parents and pleasing children in all their age groups.

By offering such facilities as night time room patrols, mothers' rooms equipped with washing machines, irons etc, and three mini clubs for different age groups of children, their company has proved successful enough to attract buyers and they are now part of the Falcon Leisure Group, the umbrella name for several holiday companies.

Iris, who started Matthews Family Holidays some 18 years ago, however, had absolutely no travel trade training. She had studied accountancy and law, subsequently very useful subjects but, at that time, she was a full-time mother, bored with only doing household chores.

> It started because we bought a couple of caravans for our own holidays in France. The twins were very young so the type of holiday was ideal, and other friends with small children often stayed, too.

It was the friends and relatives who suggested that the Matthews start renting out the caravans when they were not using them themselves.

> At the time, few people had seen the size of caravan we had, so they were very popular. We could have rented them several times over so, over the years, we gradually added more.

Eight years ago, the couple owned 50 caravans and Iris's husband could afford to give up his engineering job.

> We privately let them and arranged ferry services, first with Townsend Thoresen and then Brittany Ferries. Then I discovered there was such a thing as inclusive tour operators and we included ferry transportation in the package.

When the operation became too big to work from home, the Matthews wanted a shop in the village. However, the law said it had to be a travel agency and they had to pay to become members of the Association of British Travel Agents (ABTA) (see page 31).

> Initially, we hired a senior person but, over the years, I worked in the travel shop and learnt the business myself. As soon as our International Air Transport Association (IATA) licence (see page 32) came through, I took British Caledonian's air ticketing courses 1 and 2. These can only be taken once you're in the travel business.

At first, the holidays were advertised in newspapers such as *The Sunday Times* and a printed leaflet was sent in response to any enquiries. Twelve years ago, Matthews launched their first proper brochure. Today, there are five full-time and some 15 part-time staff (not counting those working in the agency), plus the couple themselves. And the caravans now number over 300.

Andrew took a first degree in agricultural economy and followed it up with a postgraduate course in agricultural marketing. After a couple of jobs, including several years with a regional English tourist board, he came up with a great idea for becoming a tour operator.

> Because I was working in the tourist board, I discovered there were many farmhouses in the area with rooms to let. The owners were eager for publicity but individually didn't have the financing to do it properly. What they needed was co-ordination – marketing.

That was the start of Country Farm Holidays some seven years ago; it took the form of a small brochure listing 40 farmhouses, all in the heart of England.

> Originally, I worked from home and it meant a lot of legwork, from assessing the properties, coaxing the owners to participate, to stuffing mailers into envelopes and taking bookings.

His good idea certainly worked. The programme now operates from an office with full-time staff, and the listed properties (which now include other self-catering units) number 350 and are to be found throughout the country.

Is Tour Operation Work for You?

Do you like people? Do your friends say you have a nice personality? Are you good at organising? Are you clever with ideas and following them through? Do you pay attention to detail? If you can say 'yes' to at least one of these questions, working for a tour operator or learning to become one might be the very career.

The travel industry as a whole, by its very character, is a people-orientated one. Enjoying personal travel is a start but concern for other people's needs and demands is the core of any travel-related job. At manager/director level, you would be expected to give interviews, speak on radio and/or appear on TV. You would, after all, be speaking for your own (or someone else's) company.

A public relations officer handling a travel account, either in-house or as part of a consultancy, has to be able to liaise with the managing director, the marketing department, sometimes an advertising agency, maybe the public, and always the press.

Those with titles in planning, contracts or operations have to liaise with airlines, hotels, car hire and other local ground operators to produce an acceptable and realistically priced end product. They must have enough knowledge to forecast how their product will expand while being profitable, or when to drop a particular programme. They must be aware of the competition and keep their ear to the ground in so far as the travelling public is concerned.

Travel reps and couriers are the 'upfront' members of a tour operation – those with direct contact with the public. They may well have to work unsocial hours and be prepared to deal with unexpected problems and situations.

On the other hand, those connected with finance or reservations must pay attention to detail or thousands of holidays would not work. A pleasant telephone voice and the ability to use a telex are helpful in the reservations department.

Pros and Cons

Do not expect a career in tourism to be all glamour. Yes, at top level, you will have travel benefits and an excellent salary but pressure is high. Bear in mind that most of the job opportunities in a tour operation are for travel technicians or couriers. The former is the back-room clerical variety, unlikely to be given many perks; the latter, while certainly having the chance to work abroad, does not earn a great deal for work that entails long hours, often for seven days a week.

Case Studies

Frances recently graduated from university and decided to take a year off before renewing studies, this time for accountancy. She is in her first season as a courier for Eurocamp, based in Normandy.

> Camp site couriers are usually hired on a split-season basis. That means you spend the first three months, including the setting up of tents, at one location and move on to another location for the second three months, for the taking down of tents. The season runs from April to September for part-time work like mine, and applications for employment might have to go in as early as the previous November or, in Eurocamp's case, the preceding January.
>
> Although no qualifications are specifically required, tour operators specialising in camping tend to pick university students. What you need more than anything is a pleasing personality and stamina. When a company has a good number of tents on any one site, there will be two couriers there who will have to share a tent. In my case, with only 15 tents, there's just me.
>
> In some cases, couriers will have to go through a training period or weekend briefing session, though here if you're hired after the interview, it's only a two-hour one. On the other hand, if there are complaints about your negligence to duties, you're fired immediately.
>
> When you travel out to a site in April, you travel as a team to help erect the tents, moving from site to site to do the same, dropping off respective couriers along the way. If you're in the last batch, there's more work! When I began, it took three hours for several of us to put up a tent – now I can put one up by myself in half an hour.
>
> Couriers have certain hours when they must be in their tent to answer questions or give advice to customers. During the rest of the time they're free, though you can't really say you have a day off. It can get rather lonely but you do have the chance to live abroad, improve your language of that country and you're given a moped to get around. Some of the campers are friendly and that makes it more pleasant. They'll often leave you money or a bottle of wine – certainly any left over teabags or coffee – when they depart for home.

Accommodation for camp-site couriers is naturally free, though they must pay for their own food. You can expect a salary of them) can fly from 16 UK airports on the company's own airline, Britannia Airways, or on scheduled airlines from Heathrow to long-haul destinations.

It is the marketing department which has the role of producing the holiday brochures and ensuring customer awareness of Thomson products by advertising and public relations work. The sales division operates the reservations offices and promotes and sells through travel agents. The sales force distributes several million brochures to agents.

Thomson Holidays was the first company to introduce off-season weekend breaks in resorts normally only considered for summer holidays, and winter weekends to Majorca for £18 were announced in 1971. In 1972, Thomson's offered the first charter holidays from the UK to Jamaica and introduced weekends to Moscow from £29.

In 1973, cruising was launched and summertime holidays in established lake and mountain winter resorts were offered plus a programme of long weekend breaks in European capitals. Subsequently, Thomson's expanded into winter sports.

A fair trading charter was introduced the next year – a revolutionary move in terms of booking conditions, leading the way to proper public protection. A delay protection scheme, offering cash compensation and providing hotels and meals to holiday-makers delayed at the start of their holiday, was announced for summer 1979.

Advanced systems technology to streamline sales, reservations and booking administration, is vital to every tour operator. It took three years and £3 million to develop the system Thomson's launched in 1976 when ten regional sales centres could communicate online with a powerful computer at head office via visual display units. In 1982, a reservations system called Thomson Open-Line Programme was made available to travel agents. Now over 6,000 agents are linked to the company by a TV screen using the latest Videotex technology. Direct computer links with the overseas resorts speed the administration even more and in 1987 Thomson introduced an automatic banking system (TAB) to help agents save more admin costs.

At the end of 1978, Thomson Vacations Inc was established in Chicago to market inclusive tours for Americans living in the Mid West and, in 1979, Thomson's formed a new direct-sell company – Portland Holidays. Thomson Paris was set up in 1981 for short year-round holidays; Amsterdam was added in 1983. Over the past few years, the company has further expanded into specialist fields like self-catering, coaching, golf and winter sports, and into special age ranges including schools and the elderly.

In summer 1986, Thomson almost doubled its capacity to 2.25 million holidays, cut prices by 17 per cent, promised no surcharges for the year and offered compensation money if holiday arrangements were changed. In its 11 summer 1988 brochures almost 3 million holidays are available, catering to every choice. Skytours (launched late 1987) offers the lowest prices on the market – Discount '88 cut summer holiday prices by £18 million.

Thomson Holidays has been providing inclusive holidays for 23 years, catering to over 23 million passengers during that time. Today, there are around 3,000 staff in the UK and in the resorts – planning, operating and selling Thomson holidays.

The Self-Catering Tour Operator

Putting together the elements of a self-catering holiday is relatively new, but these days very popular. A self-catering package is where travel and accommodation arrangements are included, but not food. This covers a camping or caravanning programme, or a stay in a holiday apartment or a villa. It could comprise holiday cottages in the UK, or *gîtes*, as they are called in France, or something like a Greek taverna abroad (where accommodation is basic and food is available but not included in the holiday price).

Case Study

Jim and his wife Margaret are both founders of the company Canvas Holidays, and they are both graduates of Edinburgh University. Jim gained a law degree and Margaret an MA (Hons) in history. After a spell in America, Jim returned to Scotland to join a law practice, then to the Independent Broadcasting Authority as information officer and then to Rank Bush Murphy as a marketing executive. It was only after the couple were married and worked on the fledgling Canvas Holidays operation from the dining room table, that it gradually grew into the £5 million business it is today.

By 1983, the company was offering 89 first-class camp sites, designed and developed to accommodate up to six people. Flexibility was the key with holiday-makers coming and going on any day they pleased and staying for as long as they chose. Half of the permanent staff are graduates who look after the day-to-day running at the head office in Hertfordshire. Some 350 university graduates and undergraduates are employed in the summer as couriers.

Jim and Margaret developed their business enough to establish two subsidiaries: Car Holidays Abroad in 1970, for those who preferred hotel accommodation to canvas, and Cabin Holidays in 1983, which concentrated on self-catering holidays in Scotland.

The Cuthberts (who have since been joined by their sons, now directors) have always been innovators – with their tent equipment and facilities like electric lights and toilets, to other new ideas such as their 1988 introduction of special interest camping holidays.

Here's what they say about the young people they look for to work for them:

> As a courier you are expected to be a hard worker. Every tent or mobile home has to be thoroughly cleaned before the customer arrives, and you will need to be a practical person in case any of the equipment needs to be fixed. Practical, yes, but personable, too – you can, after all, make or break a customer's holiday. Tact and diplomacy are certainly essential attributes, but so is a happy disposition. Couriers are expected to visit the on-site guests and organise informal gatherings for both adults and children such as barbecues and wine and cheese parties, as well as run the twice-weekly Hoopi Club activities (treasure hunts, rambles, sports) for the youngsters.
>
> A courier must also present a good appearance – that's why we provide the clothing for the job. Both your own tent and administration work (accounts, inventories etc) should also be in good order.
>
> We do receive thousands of applications annually for a courier's position, from whom we pick 300 either to work from the end of April to mid July, or mid July to the end of September. Our selection process starts in November and continues through June. During the November to March period, we hold regional interviews throughout Britain.
>
> What type of person do we look for? Generally speaking, an undergraduate or someone taking a year off between school or university – so mostly the age range is 18-25, but we are flexible. Fluency in French, German, Italian or Spanish is certainly an incentive to us, but even without one of these languages, there may be another job for you.
>
> The 1988 wage is £70 pw, made up of £35 salary in hand and £25 as a living allowance. The extra £10 pw is paid on completion of the contract. We should point out that during the tent setting up and taking down period (at the beginning and end of the season), we deduct £7 pw but do provide three daily meals. Your accommodation

during your contract time is obviously provided, as is the transport to and from Europe and some sort of local transport like a moped.

The same pay and conditions also apply to the children's courier whose responsibility is to look after the young ones at certain times of the day and this may include babysitting. Previous teaching, nursery school or playgroup experience is very helpful here – language fluency is not.

We also need watersports couriers – previous experience in this area is necessary, and some professional qualification is preferred. Then we need what we call 'squaddies' who don't require language knowledge but must have physical strength and stamina, be able to work long hours under some pressure and live out of a rucksack, as they are the ones who put up and take down the tents on different sites. Additionally, full-time positions as area managers are available; based in our home office, at a salary of about £10,000 pa.

Courier/Resort Rep

There are no specific qualifications for this kind of work other than personality and patience. Knowledge of at least one other language will be helpful but most tour operators hire direct and give their own intensive training programmes.

Courses

A degree course is never a bad idea, and new ones are now available in tourism at Dorset Institute of Higher Education; South Glamorgan Institute of Higher Education; Newcastle Polytechnic and New College, Durham. The University of Ulster combines tourism with catering in its BA in Hotel and Tourism Management. Many other institutions are currently developing syllabuses, and tourism options are also to be found in a number of business studies, finance, or hotel and catering administration degrees. Those who already hold a degree (whatever the subject) may opt for a postgraduate qualification in tourism at Birmingham, Strathclyde or Surry Universities, or at Manchester Polytechnic.

BTEC Courses

A number of colleges of further education offer Business and Technician Education Council (BTEC) courses in business and related studies, with an option in travel and tourism. There are three levels: BTEC General; BTEC National; and BTEC Higher National. At each level, you can choose to study for a Certificate or a Diploma. A successful pass at one level obviously means you can go on to study at a higher level.

Qualifications
To take a general level BTEC course, you must be aged 16 and have a good command of English. The Certificate course takes one year part-time, and the Diploma course one year full-time or two years part-time. To carry on for a National award, you need at least four GCE/GCSE O levels in grades A, B or C, or CSEs at grade 1, their equivalent, or a General award with credit. It is at the National and Higher National levels that you will find the travel and tourism options. They vary in duration and scope with the colleges but are designed only to give a broad (not a detailed) knowledge of the industry. Nevertheless, this award, combined with generalised business studies, is likely to be more attractive to potential employers than no qualifications at all. For further information and useful addresses, see Part 2.

CGLI Courses
Of all the tourism courses available, the most relevant to tour operation work is COTOP (Certificate of Tour Operations Practice). It is a fairly new qualification which enables you to learn how holiday packages are put together and how new technology assists.

Other Courses
Full-time, sandwich and part-time courses are offered by colleges of further and higher education, polytechnics and universities. Many companies, too, have their own training schemes.

Qualifications
The City and Guilds does not itself require any exam passes to enrol in one of its courses but some colleges featuring them will expect some GCE/GCSE passes. To take a general level BTEC course for a Certificate or Diploma, you need only be 16 with a good command of English. Most of the courses take one to two years part-time. Success in this basic grade will enable you to carry on for a National award which takes two to three years full- or part-time. Minimum requirements for direct application for a National Certificate or Diploma are three to four GCE/GCSE's with high grades. Higher National awards are possible after two to three years' study (full-time, part-time or as a sandwich course), either upon completion of National awards, or by direct

entrance at the age of 18 with a minimum of one or two A-level passes.

Grants

You may or may not be eligible for a grant to take a full-time course; your local education authority will let you know. But, when you apply for a grant, do so as early as possible. A useful booklet which is free and should be available from your school careers office or in the local library is *Grants to Students: A Brief Guide*.

Chapter 2
Travel Agencies

What is a Travel Agent?
A travel agent is someone who sells tour operators' holidays, accommodation, transportation, etc, to the general public, thus acting as an intermediary between providers and buyers. In return, the travel agent receives a commission from the tour operator.

Travel agencies may be individually owned, be part of a chain, or in some cases owned by a tour operator. Through the knowledge and experience of their personnel, they should be able to advise customers on best buys, suitable destinations and most convenient routes, as well as physically handling bookings and ticketing.

Although anyone can open a travel agency, that does not mean you can sell *any* product. Most reputable providers of holidays and holiday elements require that the agency they deal with has both an IATA licence and is an ABTA member.

What is ABTA?
The Association of British Travel Agents was formed to help protect the general public. To become a member, the agent must pay 'bond' money, a safeguard in case he/she should fall into financial failure. All ABTA members agree to comply with codes of conduct which have been drawn up by ABTA in conjunction with the Office of Fair Trading. Since these codes have been created by travel industry specialists, they cover even remote contingencies, well beyond the requirements of the law.

ABTA regularly scrutinises the finances of its members; it demands that they employ properly experienced staff and contribute to a common fund. It operates a free conciliation service which acts on behalf of a customer with a justifiable complaint, to try to find a solution acceptable to both sides. If a complaint about a package holiday does not get solved that way, ABTA can take the case to arbitration through the independent Chartered Institute of Arbitrators. (Tour operators are also usually members of ABTA and similarly abide by a code of conduct which covers matters such as procedures in the event of alterations, cancellations, surcharges or overbooking.)

What is IATA?
The International Air Transport Association is the world organisation of the scheduled airlines of over 90 nations. Members co-operate with the International Civil Aviation Organisation; they often co-ordinate international tariffs and speak with one voice in their dealings with governments and other regulatory authorities.

Travel Agent Skills

A good travel agent not only books a package holiday for a client, or writes an airline ticket, but should also be able to organise all other forms of travel arrangement, including UK holidays, business and group travel. Some travel agencies will also expect their staff to: sell travel insurance, foreign currency and travellers cheques; organise a passport or visa for a customer's trip; arrange car hire of all sorts; and possibly book theatre tickets.

A newer skill necessary is the ability to deal with computers since an increasing number of travel companies are developing their own computer systems to enable agents to make instant bookings. In many ways, this makes work easier for agency employees who can check availability and make immediate bookings direct with many tour operators, airlines, ferry companies, shipping companies, coach operators and car hire companies. The computer reservation systems enable agents to print out confirmation of a customer's booking in minutes so that the customer may take it away with them instead of waiting to receive it through the post. Additionally, some of the computer systems can automatically suggest alternative holidays or call up extra information, such as insurance details, and show the full price before the booking is made.

Where Can You Go?

A travel agency is the ideal place to start if you are planning a career in tourism. Vacancies for counter clerks and travel technicians (who put into effect the bookings made by the counter clerks) offer job opportunities for school-leavers from the age of 16. At that age, you would be employed to handle the simpler aspects of the work, progressing to the more complex operational work as you gain experience. Larger travel agencies employ staff with qualifications and experience in accountancy, marketing and advertising and offer considerable prospects at their head offices for personnel with other professional and academic qualifications.

You might work towards becoming the manager of a single agency, several agencies, your own agency, or in time move to operations at head office with the eventual idea of becoming a company director (or managing director) or moving sideways into a tour operation.

Jobs and promotion will obviously go to those people with the right training, ability, appearance, personality and motivation. At any job interview, ask what training you will be given; for example, if you are 16 or 17, will the employer put you on the ABTA youth training course or, if you are older, will you be given training for the Certificate of Travel Agency Competence (COTAC) and an opportunity to sit the exams and become qualified?

Salaries are variable depending on location, your expected responsibilities as well as experience.

Case Studies

Kate has just joined a London travel agency as a trainee travel clerk.

> After I left school, I took a two-year full-time travel and tourism course at Thurrock College. Qualifications for this are five O levels but if you wish to take the higher course, which is bilingual, you need at least two A levels, one of which must be a foreign language.
>
> Thurrock has a very good reputation so a number of agencies will call when they have vacancies for juniors. At present, I'm mostly involved with air ticketing but I shall be working on inclusive tours and other elements for which I've been trained. I'm not sure what my ultimate aim is but a travel and tourism course does open a variety of doors in the travel industry, when it's followed by some practical experience.

Julie, at only 19, has the title of travel consultant at a travel agency which is not ABTA- or IATA-licensed.

> I got my first job with a travel agency at 17. I only had one O level in

English and some CSEs because my father is in the Forces and we'd moved about a great deal. How did I do it? I got out the *Yellow Pages* and listed every travel agency near where I lived – then I wrote to them all, asking if they had a position for a trainee. Most just sent applications forms or said they'd let me know if something turned up, but one man was interested enough to call me for an interview. I think he was surprised I had showed initiative and I was employed to do some typing and background bookings work.

Whatever you do you learn about the travel business and I was particularly interested in travel sales. When another employee opened her own company – The Trans-Continental Travel Company – she took me along with her. Because we are not ABTA-licensed, you might call us a 'bucket shop', but bucket shops generally are so called because they buy tickets in bulk and sell them off cheaply. We, on the other hand, specialise in independent travel, particularly around the world. When someone calls me up with where they want to go, I let them know the best routing and cheapest way of doing it, and organise their bookings. Our holding company, by the way, is ABTA/IATA so customers are reassured.

Qualifications

Basic qualifications are several GCE/GCSE O level passes including English language, mathematics and geography, but a knowledge of one or more European languages is an advantage. The ability to write legibly with careful attention to detail, speak well and answer telephone enquiries personably and efficiently, are also assets. Accuracy with figures is important and a pleasant manner and interest in people, a must.

Courses

ABTA Youth Training Scheme

From time to time, the Association of British Travel Agents arranges 12-month training courses combined with work experience in the travel industry, at a number of centres throughout the country. This is aimed at 16- to 17-year-olds who seek employment in the travel trade, and provides training up to COTAC level 1 examination standards. No promise of permanent employment is made, but each ABTA-sponsored trainee on the scheme receives a weekly training allowance plus some help with travel expenses. There are some 25 regional training centres handling about 1,000 young people annually.

How can you apply? Either after a tour operator or travel

of around £45 to £70 a week which is generally paid into an English bank in sterling.

Nick graduated from university with a degree in French and Spanish. Not knowing which career he really wanted, he joined Eurocamp as a courier and was very quickly promoted to his present position as field supervisor.

> I oversee about 11 sites in my region which means I'm constantly on the move (in a car paid for by the company) and living out of a suitcase. I think of my base as Paris, but in fact I have no permanent tent as the couriers do.
>
> Supervisors check that everything is running smoothly on the sites and that the couriers are doing their job. But they're also around to help when difficult problems arise. Any of the couriers can call me any time when there's a tricky situation, and I'm on my way.

Problems that call for a supervisor might include a site that is flooded out and requires evacuation and re-placement of holiday-makers; a stolen passport; or a death on the site when red tape and emotion have to be coped with. Nick is a full-time employee, returning to the headquarters office for the winter months. His expectations are to move into planning or operations areas with this or a larger company. A field supervisor's salary is likely to be in the £8,000 pa bracket with four weeks' holiday a year, two at high season, to return home to England.

Jan is currently a full-time employee of Twentys Holidays with the title overseas co-ordinator. Now 24 years old, she started this career on a part-time level, as a courier.

> No specific qualifications are required for courier work providing someone is literate and numerate. You don't even need a foreign language though I'm not saying it isn't a help. Personality and style plus stamina count for far more, especially since Twentys deals with the youth market and couriers are expected very much to join in.
>
> The company starts looking at applications for summer work around October/November and first-stage interviews are given around the country. Selected interviewees are then invited to Hereford over a weekend to participate in a second-stage interview when a number of tasks (indoors and out) are set – to do individually and as a team. Twentys tries to make them 'unexpected' but they certainly include being kept up to the early hours.

Twentys couriers have to be aged 20 to 33 to match the market and are hired for the summer season – at its longest, April to October. Some may be given winter work if they wish it and if it is available. Some, if they do well and wish it, will be rehired for the following summer season. A few might be required to work in the winter months at the head office. Once at a destination, accommodation and any food that the hotel includes are free. One week's holiday is given when possible but there is no guarantee of even a day off during any given week. Generally, several couriers are assigned to one group of clients. They are expected not only to deal with problems, but to organise games and outings and drink with the best! (Being quite as sociable is not true for all travel company reps and couriers.)

Jan's first position was as assistant courier, then courier, senior courier and then resort manager.

> My present job involves co-ordinating staff movements, progress and training from a headquarters base. I would only be liable to travel to resorts once or twice a year and only then to sort something out.

The Giant Tour Operators

Without delving into the history of every major tour operator, let us just look at one giant and its background – Thomson Holidays, Britain's largest inclusive tour operator.

Thomson Holidays is part of Thomson Travel Ltd, the travel and holiday division of the International Thomson Organisation Ltd, which also controls newspapers and magazines, publishing, North Sea oil and other world-wide interests. The travel division itself operates its own airline, tour operating companies and a travel agency group.

When SkyTours, Riviera Holidays, Gaytours and Luxitours were amalgamated in the 1960s, they eventually formed Thomson SkyTours in 1970, which then became Thomson Holidays in 1972. That same year, the company acquired Sunair and Lunn Poly and the latter now operates over 350 retail travel outlets under the Lunn Poly name.

The continental department of Thomson Holidays looks after all aspects of overseas holidays. It is responsible for contracting aircraft and the accommodation used and provides those necessary services such as reps, baby patrollers, airport transfers and excursions. In high season, there are over 2,000 staff overseas, trained by this department. Quality control is also an important part of the continental department's work – monitoring all aspects of a holiday with the help of client-completed questionnaires.

Thomson passengers (in 1987 there were more than 6 million

agency has hired you, or by writing to request an interview to the Administrator, ABTA Youth Training Scheme, ABTA National Training Board, 11-17 Chertsey Road, Woking, Surrey GU21 5AL. (Personal enquiries or telephone calls about the scheme cannot be dealt with.)

COTAC

The Certificate of Travel Agency Competence (COTAC) is widely accepted throughout the trade and acquiring it should be one of your priorities. Level 1 may be taken after one year's employment experience, and level 2 after two and a half years' work experience. COTAC training is included in the ABTA youth training scheme, but the City and Guilds of London Institute (CGLI) in conjunction with ABTA runs exams, the successful completion of which leads to COTAC.

The CGLI also offers a full-time course in Travel Studies (reference number 499). Students who successfully complete this are considered to have completed COTAC 1 and indeed some subjects for COTAC 2.

BTEC

A full-time Business and Technician Education Council (BTEC) National Diploma course may be your way into the travel trade. Courses can incorporate up to six travel option modules: travel and tourism 1 and 2; travel geography; retail travel operations; tour operations; and sales and marketing for travel and tourism.

Apply to those colleges which use the combination of modules to suit your requirements. Some, by the way, also include periods of work experience, UK visits and specialised ticketing examinations. For details of colleges running such courses, write to BTEC, Central House, Upper Woburn Place, London WC1H 0HH. If you live in Scotland, you should write to SCOTVEC, 24 Douglas Street, Glasgow G2 7NG; the Scottish Vocational Education Council was formed in 1985 to design modular courses which would replace City and Guilds or similar courses, although as both have agreed on a system of equivalences, students who complete a SCOTVEC National Certificate may also be awarded a CGLI qualification.

ABTA Seal of Approval Courses

Within a two-year full-time BTEC National Diploma course, there should be 12 modules of which six are compulsory 'core' subjects. In order to get the ABTA seal of approval, a college operating this course must include at least five of the newly designed travel and tourism modules. The final module can either be the sixth travel module or could be any other standard module which the college provides.

The ABTA National Training Board has produced a list of colleges and other establishments which have been awarded the seal. To obtain it, send a stamped addressed envelope to the Education and Training Adviser, ABTA National Training Board, 11-17 Chertsey Road, Woking, Surrey GU21 5AL.

A Higher National award can well lead to management and then it might be worthwhile proving your skills by taking COTAM, another ABTA certificate of competence.

Approved BTEC qualifications, COTAC or COTAM all admit membership to the Institute of Travel and Tourism.

For details of training colleges and institutions offering travel courses, see Part 2.

Other Courses
There are several education centres which offer recognised courses in various aspects of the travel industry. The Hotel and Travel Training College, for example, was established in the 1960s. It is a private training institute whose syllabus covers a number of subjects necessary to travel agency work. These include computer instruction, British Airways fares and ticketing courses, and general travel. Although these courses do not come cheaply, the advantage for young people is that they are intense and do not always require as many GCE/GCSE qualifications as might colleges of further education.

The 1988 college syllabus includes:

British Airways Basic Airline Course
The objectives of this are to: define IATA areas and IATA three-letter city codes; plan itineraries for any journey, giving accurate information about timings, connections, baggage allowances, aircraft types and airport facilities, flying times and red tape requirements; calculate fares for single or multi-sector journeys both within the UK and abroad, and issue appropriate tickets; handle bookings for special categories of passenger, eg, pregnant mothers, invalids, unaccompanied minors, etc.

Fares and Ticketing Course 1
The objectives of this course are: to use the air tariff to quote all kinds of fares in local currency, for one-way, round trip, circle

trip, open jaw, etc, using add-ons, certain routings, mileage system, etc; to use IATA-approved procedures to issue tickets for journeys of four-flight sectors or less.

Selling for Starters
A course that is intended for travel agency staff who need to know the basic principles of selling, but have not had any previous sales experience. (The school suggests this should be taken in conjunction with the British Airways basic airline course.)

Travel Geography
A mostly visual geography lesson with co-operation from tourist boards.

General Travel
In addition to the travel sales module, instruction is given to students on general counter duties, tour operator costings, grounding in car hire booking, hotel reservations and coach booking procedures.

Rail Travel
The course has been designed so that, on completion, students are able to prepare journeys by rail anywhere in the world using the *ABC Rail Guide* and the Thomas Cook International Timetable. This course also includes the Sealink continental fares and ticketing course covering reservations, layout of continental rolling stock, fares compilation, ticket issue, etc.

Sea Travel
Students will study the *ABC Shipping Guide* in detail together with literature of the main cruise operators. During the course, they will experience a car ferry trip at first-hand and at the end of it will sit the car ferries exam.

Coach Travel
The training personnel from National Travel supervise this course which covers all aspects of scheduled services throughout mainland Britain plus overseas services. Instruction is given on routes, reservation procedures, facilities, sales aids and potential markets. Those who pass the exam will obtain the National Travel certificate.

Fares and Ticketing Course 2

Only open to those who have already successfully passed course 1. This is designed for those planning to sit the COTAC level 2 airline paper. Features include: applying the fare construction principles learnt in course 1 plus calculating mixed class fares; determining the correct type of excursion or special fare for any routing; correctly applying round and circle trip construction rules to world-wide excursion and other special fares; applying rebates for child, infant, youth and student fares; amending flight, date, destination and/or stopover details by using revalidation slips or by re-issuing tickets; and applying the correct currency procedures should the re-routing result in an additional fare collection (in sterling or other currencies).

The Blue Riband Course

Open only to 18 students at a time (who must be aged 18 and have a minimum of three O levels), this is a particularly intense nine-week course covering all aspects of travel as contained in the other separate courses.

NB. The 1988 cost of the above course was £625.

Another private education centre offering travel training is the Belair Education Centre, 10 Denmark Street, London WC2H 8LS; tel 01-379 7510, where full-time or evening courses are available. Applicants must be aged at least 16 and have a sound general education.

The airline courses (officially approved by British Airways, ABTA and the Institute of Travel and Tourism) are two weeks full-time or ten weeks by evening classes. (1988 costs were £195.) A pass mark obtains both the official BA certificate and a Belair certificate.

Chapter 3
Hotels

Hotels play a very big part in the travel industry. Tour operators must contract with them; travel agencies must book them. Tourists, business and conference groups all use them. Hotelkeeping and catering itself is one of the country's largest industries employing at least two million men and women in UK establishments alone, thereby offering a multitude of job opportunities at all levels.

Hotelkeeping and catering is an international industry that includes job opportunities at airports, in leisure centres and holiday camps, convention centres and exhibition halls both at home and abroad. There is also a demand for catering by transport systems such as airlines, trains and cruise ships.

What Qualifications are Needed?

Depending upon which aspect you choose, you may need anything from no qualifications to a degree in hotel management. GCSEs or their equivalents are always an advantage but they are not essential for entry into cookery, waiting, housekeeping, reception or a general catering course. They are, however, a must for management occupations, and the most helpful subjects are English language or literature, mathematics, science and any foreign language.

The Hotel and Catering Training Board itself offers craft achievement awards in cookery, food service, reception and housekeeping to young people already employed. In this case you will attend college on day-release in the employer's time and receive a craft award upon completion of industrial experience.

Youth Training Scheme

A basic 12-month foundation training programme is offered by the Board with a minimum of three months' off-the-job training or related further education. Trainees will be encouraged to obtain at least two City and Guilds of London Institute (CGLI) specific skills qualifications during the year. Job possibilities under this scheme include room attendants, grill chefs, receptionists, cashiers and jobs in the stores or maintenance departments.

Picking the Right Area

Do you like people? Do you have no difficulty chatting and do you smile easily? Are you flexible and enthusiastic? Are you pleased with your personality and appearance? If the answers to these questions are 'yes', any of the careers where you meet the general public could be for you – that includes jobs at the reception desk and in the press office.

Are you academically terrible but good with your hands? Are you creative but shy? You do not have to be out in front for a position that involves cooking.

Do you love attention to detail, neatness and tidyness? A position in accounts, stores or stock-taking could be your answer. Or perhaps you may be best working for a hotel group or reservations system making bookings.

The possibilities are as endless as the prospects. If you are really not quite sure of which area to specialise in, take a general course first such as the City and Guilds 705 General Catering course which provides school-leavers with an introduction to the industry. This is a one-year full-time course, often taken as the first year of a two-year full-time craft course.

The Chef

There are all kinds of chefs working in all kinds of establishments, but there is no specific route to the top. You could get a job as an apprentice or trainee chef when you leave school, in which case you would probably attend a local college on day-release for formal as well as practical training. Alternatively, you might opt for a two-year full-time training course to become a commis chef (assistant).

What Courses?

CGLI's 706-1 Cookery for the Catering Industry Part 1 and 706-2 Cookery for the Catering Industry Part 2 are both nationally recognised qualifications in food preparation and cookery. These may be taken by trainees on day-release or on block-release (working normally but attending college for several weeks at a time), over a three-year period, or full-time over two years.

Advanced courses are the CGLI 706-3 Certificate; CGLI 771 Organisation Studies (catering) and the supervisory courses of the National Examinations Board for Supervisory Studies and the Scottish Vocational Education Council (SCOTVEC).

Cookery for the Catering Industry Part 3 supplies specialist knowledge in kitchen and larder plus pastry. The course is available to those who have passed CGLI 706-2 and have five years' practical experience (for kitchen and larder specialism), or four years' practical experience (pastry specialism).

Case Studies
Nick left school seven years ago to become an apprentice in a large hotel kitchen. He is now *sous* chef (assistant to the head chef).

> Initially, I was on day-release at a local technical college for the formal part of my training. To be a chef, you must not only love cooking but be prepared for long hours, often on shift, to work hard and cope with hassles. In my present brigade (team of chefs) there are 12 people to cope with banqueting and restaurant meals. My job involves running the kitchen, from checking the supplies to planning the menus for the next month together with the head chef. I supervise all the duties that need to be done in order to have food ready for service, though my special responsibility is training the *commis* chef and apprentices.

Nick still has to work a split shift and some weekends, though some hotels have two brigades. His eventual aim is to open his own restaurant.

The Waiter/Waitress

Food and beverage service will keep you very much in the public eye for longer periods than in any other type of catering work. Although no qualifications are compulsory, if you have an eye to job prospects in wine waiting or food and beverage management, training is essential.

What Courses?
Food and Beverage Service Part 1 (CGLI 707-1) gives an introduction to the industry and the basic knowledge and skills necessary to develop a career. Food and Beverage Service Part 2

(CGLI 707-2) is an advanced course that teaches final preparation of foods at a side table or trolley and includes function catering and organisation of food and beverage service. Completion of this should lead to a position as head waiter/waitress.

Alcoholic Beverages Certificate (CGLI 717) teaches skills concerned with selling and serving wines and other alcoholic beverages.

Case Study
Kelvin is currently a master *sommelier* or wine waiter in a plush restaurant.

> I got a job as a waiter with no qualifications at all, but I was interested in wine so studied in my own time and took several exams set by the Guild of Sommeliers. To become a 'master *sommelier*' is to pass their top exam. I also hope to take a full-time hotel management course. At the moment, I work a split shift seven days a week. At the beginning of each duty spell, I check the stock of wines and see that the tables are properly laid with clean glasses and ashtrays. Service includes cocktails as well as wines and then liqueurs. A knowledge of food is helpful and enjoying people, essential. We are lucky here having two wine waiters and a *commis*, but in small restaurants, you would be expected to wash glasses and clean up yourself.

The Receptionist

A hotel receptionist may be one of a team of 20 or so working a rota system, checking customers in and out along with other duties that may include book-keeping, handling cash and foreign exchange, taking reservations and dealing with accounts. Large hotels do sometimes employ staff aged under 18 in a junior capacity, but since front office work is responsible, 18 is usually the minimum age.

What Courses?
Recommended for 16-year-old school-leavers is the CGLI one-year full-time 709 hotel reception certificate (though it is sometimes offered on a block-release basis). It covers not only reception, but hotel organisation, bookkeeping and office practice, and is offered at a variety of colleges which may ask for two or three GCE/GCSE passes for entry.

SCOTVEC organises a National Certificate for hotel receptionists which includes typing, but since it is a modular course there are several optional subjects. Students with reasonable exam pass grades are eligible for this full-time course available at many colleges of further education.

You could find a secretarial course helpful before considering hotel reception work and a BTEC National qualification in front office operations is extremely useful as are both the BTEC and SCOTVEC National qualification in business studies.

Case Study
Jeannie took a full-time reception course on leaving school and is currently head receptionist in a large city hotel.

> How quickly you get promotion depends a little on luck and the size of the establishment. Turnover in this work is fast, however, so if you prove you are good, you can become a head receptionist quite quickly, as I did. In my job I am responsible for all the front office staff work – that includes the other receptionists, telephonists and reservations clerks. I organise the staff rota and help to select and train new staff.
>
> You need a good personality and appearance; a good telephone manner – and patience. Its disadvantages are the long hours that can be disastrous for your social life; problems with guests – there are always some who cause problems, but you can't be rude; and headaches if accounts don't balance. The advantage is that no two days are ever alike!

The Housekeeper

This is a job for a practical person who enjoys responsibility but does not seek to meet the public. You might start off as a junior or trainee in a large hotel straight from school, or you might work your way up from chambermaid (but this is a slow process). Promotion for a keen enthusiastic person can soon lead to a head housekeeping position when you will need to work closely with the reception and maintenance staff and supervise fully employed and casual room cleaning labour.

What Courses?
The CGLI 708 Accommodation Services Certificate may be taken as a one-year full-time course, or as part-time or on block-release. Subjects covered include: operational procedures; organisation and work of linen rooms; laundry; security; and safety and hygiene.

Case Study

Rona joined a large northern hotel as a trainee housekeeper and took her CGLI 708 on block-release. She is currently one of three assistant housekeepers.

> Housekeeping duties vary according to establishment and numbers of full-time staff. Here, in addition to a head housekeeper and two other assistants, we have 13 room cleaners. I work on a rota system with my two colleagues which sometimes means starting the day as early as 6.30 am. If a chambermaid is away, it might mean cleaning rooms, too!
>
> The most important element of the day is collecting the rooming sheet from reception which tells me which rooms have been occupied the night before and which guests are leaving that day. Linen checks are a must – for the current and following day. So are empty room checks – to make sure they have been cleaned properly, and that lights and other fixtures work. Reservations have to be checked for special requirements like flowers or champagne in the room or a cot. We also deal with guests' special requests like hair dryers or irons. A housekeeper needs to know a great deal about cleaning methods such as removing coffee or wine stains from carpets and curtains.

The Manager

Managers are needed in every department in a hotel from front office to food and beverage division. To become a general manager, you would usually have to have worked in several of the departments at top level first.

There are a number of different courses available to the potential management trainee from degree courses down. To become a manager you need a consuming interest and full commitment.

What Courses?
BTEC
Colleges of further and higher education offer programmes in hotel and catering subjects validated by the Business and Technician Education Council (BTEC). These have replaced Ordinary and Higher National Diploma (OND and HND) courses. Programmes are modular and students take a number of units which build into a Certificate or Diploma. BTEC Certificate in Hotel, Catering and Institutional Operations is normally a part-time programme.

BTEC Diploma in Hotel, Catering and Institutional Operations is normally offered on a two-year full-time basis.
BTEC Higher Certificate in Hotel, Catering and Institutional Management is normally part-time.
BTEC Higher Diploma in Hotel, Catering and Institutional Management is usually on a full-time sandwich basis over two to three years. 'Direct entry' students with A levels take bridging units.

You will need some GCE/GCSE passes to take the BTEC courses or their Scottish equivalent. Direct entry to Higher Diploma programmes requires at least one A level pass.

HCIMA Courses
The aim of the Hotel, Catering and Institutional Management Association courses is to provide a basic knowledge of all aspects of hotelkeeping and catering. The HCIMA courses are in two parts: Part A is offered on a part-time basis over two years and part B on a one-year full-time basis, after appropriate industrial experience, as a two-year sandwich course, or as a three-year part-time course. A list of colleges offering these courses may be obtained from HCIMA, 191 Trinity Road, London SW17 7HN; tel: 01-672 4251.

Case Studies
Geoff has worked in hotels of all kinds and at all levels before reaching his present position as manager of a large city centre hotel.

> I joined a hotel chain straight from school and spent six years training, going through all the departments. I spent three subsequent years abroad in different countries before returning to the UK. Then I spent two more years in British hotels before joining this one five years ago. It usually takes a long time to reach top management level and these days much of my work is administrative.
>
> Under me there's a deputy manager, an assistant manager, a personnel officer, food and beverage manager and banqueting manager. They are all heads of department but I oversee their work. There are no set hours when you're a hotel manager – it depends on what work is at hand. The day usually starts with the post and the duty manager's report on the previous night's occupancy and any problems that might have arisen. There's usually a daily meeting for heads of departments but, apart from that, each day is completely different. Though I delegate work, in the end it's my responsibility.

Martin chose quite a different area of management, and is currently assistant manager at a motorway service area.

> When I left school, I did a two-year full-time junior management course in hotel and catering studies. Then I went into hotel management for two years prior to coming here. The hours now are regular ones although I do have to work many weekends and sometimes visit night shifts. The rest of the staff work a split shift as we're open 24 hours a day, seven days a week. Because we're in the commercial fast food business – people don't come here for an expensive meal – there's a different set of organisational problems from those in a hotel, but the job's a challenge I enjoy.

Sales and Marketing

The careers we've talked about so far in the hotel industry are all 'operational', but another large area is sales and marketing. Every hotel has a sales team and hotel chains additionally have group sales and marketing departments, both on a national and, when appropriate, international level. A large hotel is likely to employ its own public relations or press officer and here, again, international chains will also have a group public relations office.

Qualifications for this side of the industry are the same initially as for any other industry: an aggressive, positive attitude; precise and forward thinking; a smart appearance and likeable manner. There are numerous sales and marketing courses available. One of your best bets is to read *Careers in Marketing, Advertising and Public Relations* in the same series.

Hotel Group Marketing

How does this relate to the travel industry? Many hotel groups or consortiums produce their own holiday packages, especially in the UK. These are then sold through travel agents to the public just like any inclusive programme. In a case like this, the hotels' marketing team works closely with transportation (car hire companies or perhaps British Rail) and with the print and production team to produce annual brochures.

The Hotel Consortium

'Consortium' is the name given to a group of unrelated hotels (ie, usually independently owned) who generally cannot afford their own sales/reservations office. By becoming what in effect is a group, they can save time and money and make more of an impact on the market. Bookings for any of the members are taken in one place. Marketing and public relations efforts for all and any members stem from one office.

More often than not, member hotels will have something in common. Perhaps they are all country house hotels or historic house hotels. Perhaps they have a certain luxury standard (as with Prestige) or maybe they are all inns.

Hotel Group Reservations

Large international hotels have their own reservation service. Others will use a world-wide reservations service such as Utell. In almost all cases, training is done in-house. What qualifications should you have when you apply for a reservations job? Certainly, a good educational background is necessary (Hilton Reservations Service looks for young peoople with a minimum of four GCE/GCSEs). A general knowledge of geography is important since you will be dealing with reservations for places around the globe and any previous hotel background is helpful in understanding the product and possible booking problems.

You will be on the telephone a lot so a pleasant conversational manner is necessary and, since you may well be talking to executives, a mature and efficient sounding approach is equally essential. These days, 99 per cent of reservation offices use computers so a basic computer course is beneficial. But, remember that each hotel group has its own procedures so that, as Hilton Reservations Service points out, a person trained in Sheraton reservations will have to be retrained for Hilton.

Hotel Representation

Hotels which do not have their own reservations or sales office may choose a hotel representative to act on their behalf. Hotel representation, as opposed to a straightforward booking service, invariably involves public relations, sales and marketing as well as reservation taking, so that job prospects are better and career choice more exciting. The hotel representative will only take on hotels of a similar nature or alternatively concentrate on a particular part of the world. Work involves liaison with tour operators, travel agencies, the press and the individual hotels themselves.

Other Means

In addition to the recognised colleges and courses, private

education centres also offer relevant training. But don't forget, many hotel chains train within - at all levels, even from the bottom up. Crest Hotels, for example, is a British-based hotel company moving from strength to strength. It runs development courses for graduates, to prepare them for a management position. It runs a three-year programme to train students for a responsible kitchen position in a Crest hotel. It runs what is usually a nine-month training period for the front office. Depending upon what level is being aimed for, Crest looks for the following qualifications: a hotel and catering or tourism degree; a BTEC Higher National Diploma; an HCIMA qualification; a postgraduate diploma in hotel-related studies; a City and Guilds 706, Parts 1 and 2; and a City and Guilds 708, Parts 1 and 2.

Chapter 4
Airlines

So you want to work with the airlines, but where do you start? There are many areas from operational to administrative. Engineering, catering, or sales could all lead to an airline career. You could become a pilot, a steward/stewardess or work at an airport. Or you could take telephone reservations or meet and greet VIPs. Many of these jobs involve shift work, for which the minimum age is 18.

Administration

British and foreign airlines run administrative offices in the UK. They all employ telephonists, receptionists and secretaries. They all have a sales manager and/or sales team, plus a marketing manager and/or marketing division. In some cases they will have their own public relations office; in others they will use the services of an outside public relations agency. They all liaise with an advertising agency and operate a ticketing office.

Airline headquarters in the UK have personnel, financial and promotional divisions and, in cases like British Airways and British Caledonian, their own tour operation sectors. All major carriers have their own ticket desks at Heathrow and/or Gatwick.

Operations

In addition to those who fly and work on the planes, there is airport work. The airports have their own administrative teams too, of course, but ground handling might mean anything from meeting a celebrity off a flight to handling groups or unaccompanied children, or coping with an emergency.

Catering also comes under the operational banner – in the

airport itself and for the airlines. And cargo handling is yet another possibility.

The Steward/Stewardess

This is probably the easiest job to obtain in the airline world, but even so there are hundreds of applications for just one vacancy. Luckily for job hunters, the turnover is high so write to as many airlines as possible, applying to be trained. (Airlines train their own stewards and stewardesses.)

Entry requirements for cabin crew vary slightly with the airline but usually they require a minimum height of between 5ft 2in and 5ft 4in; a pleasing appearance with weight in proportion to height; and an education that includes some GCE/GCSEs. Successful applicants must also pass a medical. Good English and reasonable ability in at least one other language is certainly a help and any previous experience in nursing, teaching or catering is beneficial.

The thought of seeing and staying in destinations you could never afford gives a cabin crew career its glamour, but in fact it is not quite the glamorous job you might think. People who tell you that it is 'glorified waiting' are only too right. There is the benefit of travel, but not every route takes you to an exotic destination and not every stopover is long enough to enjoy it. Flying so frequently can upset the bodily system (particularly for women) and even when you are not flying, you may be 'on call', ie, available for work at a moment's notice. Working unpredictable hours can also play havoc with any social life.

The airlines run their own full-time training courses for newly accepted staff, which may last up to six weeks. During that time such subjects as galley management, customer relations, first aid and emergency procedures are covered, as well as the serving of food and beverages. Advanced training usually follows after several months' flight experience and refresher courses are given from time to time.

Case Study

Tracy works as a stewardess on domestic and short haul flights to Europe.

> Training is quite involved. You learn emergency procedures, cabin service and first aid. I was even shown how to survive in the desert and the Arctic. At the end of the course there's an exam which

requires a 96 per cent pass mark. If the airline flies several different types of aircraft, each with its own procedures, you must learn all of them. You must also know the duties of each member of the cabin crew so that, in an emergency, you could take over from them. Every year there's a refresher course, a line check on each aircraft and a spot check.

On short flights, you rarely get to stay anywhere since you're out on one flight and back on the next, but working in the airline business does give us opportunities to buy cheaper holidays. It's really harder work on short flights when you maybe only have an hour to serve over 70 passengers with drinks and food. Galley space is minimal so you need to keep everything neat and tidy. Number one stewardesses also have to do quite a bit of paperwork - an element of the job that trainees sometimes forget.

Reservations and Ticketing

Airlines, like other travel organisations, tend to train their own staff for reservations and ticketing procedures. These days, one of the most important factors is the ability to work with computers.

Case Study

Jennie until recently worked for South African Airlines in reservations, though the airline sent her on a ticketing course.

> I started my career with no formal training, leaving school at 16 with some O levels to work at Thomas Cook. They asked me what I wanted to do and I told them 'a booking clerk'. But all the other school-leavers wanted to do the same and being the most junior, I had to start my way at the bottom as a mail clerk. In a large organisation like Cook's, there are many areas for promotion. I moved to being a debitor, then an itinerary clerk, then an individual inclusive itinerary clerk - checking a traveller's itinerary, making bookings for hotels, car hire, etc. I left Cook's to join the reservations team at Middle East Airlines who trained on the spot. At that time it was a manual system. Then I went on to South African Airways where I was retrained in computer systems.

Ground Staff

When airlines recruit ground staff they look for people aged between 20 and 30, and used to dealing with the general public. They must have a general standard of GCE/GCSE education and since it (like cabin staff) is a uniformed job, weight must be in proportion to height. Another language is helpful. Successful applicants then go on a four-week in-house training course. Since an airline like BA promotes from within, many ground staff (including the special unit which handles VIPs, etc) are recruited from former air hostesses.

Case Study

Tessa until recently was a stewardess with Britannia Airways and has now moved to the administration unit as ground staff.

> My stewardess job was my first since school; I got the job by applying to an ad in the paper. They required English O level and two other O levels. After sending in an application with photo, I was called with several others for an interview. They talked to us individually about our family and social life and then gave us a simple maths test. After that they split us into small groups to work on an imaginary plan of campaign involving travel arrangements. If you pass all that and your weight and measurements are all right, you also have to take a medical before you are taken on as a trainee.

In Tessa's case, the course was a three-week one that included first aid (with an exam) and training for emergencies and cabin sales before she 'got her wings'.

> You start as a three or four - ie, there's a number one head stewardess who takes care of most of the paperwork; a number two who does the customs paperwork and then a three or four. For the first three flights, a really senior stewardess checks you out and, for the first three months, you're subject to constant assessments. We worked on a roster so we knew three weeks in advance which routes we were on - either in the UK or abroad, averaging a stopover only once in six weeks.

Tessa's current job is as co-ordinator checking the assessments of new girls.

Working at Airports

Not all the airports are the same so jobs can vary as can titles. In some cases, it is the airport operator who is the employer (for management, administration, baggage handling, maintenance, cleaning, information, apron control, medical and emergency services). Other employers may be private companies based at an airport (careers here might include catering, car hire, etc).

Airline traffic staff need at least four GCE/GCSEs and must be over 18. Some airlines offer a general training scheme which

Airlines

encompasses accounts, cargo, reservations, passenger services, computer operations and personnel. In most cases, airlines offer four-year maintenance engineering apprenticeships.

Competition for an air traffic control position is fierce. The Civil Aviation Authority (CAA) has a Cadet Entry Scheme for which candidates must be aged 18 to 26 and have at least two A levels. Cadets are selected by tests and interviews. Entry into Customs and Excise or immigration careers is by the Civil Service entry exam.

The British Airports Authority recruits graduates for training in computing, finance and management services and the CAA sometimes recruits people with previous experience in airport operation, for managerial positions. If your aim is to become an airport manager, you might consider some of the BTEC and SCOTVEC Higher National Diplomas in business studies which include transport options. Degree courses in transport administration, management and planning are offered by a number of universities and polytechnics.

Chapter 5
Tourist Offices

What is a Tourist Office?

A tourist office is a country's representative abroad whose main function is to provide the general public with information regarding that country. Other functions involve working with airlines, travel agents, hotels, stores and the media for promotional activities. Most major countries support a tourist office in the UK.

The director (and deputy if any) is almost always a native of the country represented, as is the majority of the staff – though the latter may live permanently in the UK. In some cases, the director might stay for years in the same post but, more frequently, he/she is in a term of office for three or four years before being relocated.

Career Opportunities

A number of tourist offices employ a public relations officer who may or may not originally be from the country being represented. If not, a knowledge of the language is almost always demanded. Sometimes an outside public relations agency will be used, in which case language may not be a requisite. Also, a tourist office generally uses an advertising agency and sometimes will have its own publications department. In a few cases, there may even be a conference or business group specialist.

The main job opportunities for British school-leavers, however, are as secretaries or counter staff (information officers) and, of course, telephonists. Secretarial skills apart, there is no defined way of entry to work in a foreign tourist office, though obviously a knowledge of the country concerned is going to give you an edge.

The British Tourist Authority

The British Tourist Authority's (BTA) prime job is to promote Britain to overseas visitors. The main function is, therefore, marketing within which there are other divisions: business, incentive and conference travel; a press and public relations office; film and TV and radio division; production services; publications; and distribution.

With the exception of clerical staff, most of the people working here are specialists in their field, though their backgrounds are extremely diversified. Journalistic or marketing experience is frequently desirable.

National Tourist Boards

The National Tourist Boards' function is to promote their own country to visitors so, like the BTA, the main role of the English, Irish, Scottish and Welsh Tourist Boards is marketing. Under this heading come departments like planning and research, and sales and distribution as well as sectors which deal with publications, the press and the travel trade.

A division called special facilities handles promotions and events while the external relations division liaises with the regional tourist boards and their own press and public relations. Special projects and finance come under a research and development banner, and central services involve personnel, office services, computerised operations and information officers.

The English Tourist Board

The English Tourist Board (ETB) is particularly enthusiastic about promoting jobs in the tourist industry. It has its own education and training department at 25 Grosvenor Gardens in London, and publishes, as part of its information service, several helpful careers information sheets for school-leavers from age 16 to university graduate age. The *Handbook of Tourism and Leisure* (published for the ETC) is also a useful acquisition for anyone with an eye on a career in this industry.

Regional Tourist Boards

Britain is split into a number of regions, each of which boasts its own tourist board – a division of the ETB. Work involves marketing that specific region with the aid of promotions, publicity, events and sometimes conference services. Staffing is not large and competition for vacancies, when they arise, is stiff.

Tourist Information Centres

Tourist information centres are scattered throughout the UK in places of visitor importance. They may range from a small centrally located kiosk to an office with several employees. These are the places to which the general public comes seeking information – where to stay or eat, how to get to a certain attraction or site, what events are taking place that day, etc. The information office may produce its own written material for tourist guidance, but is more likely to act as a distributor. Staff are generally locals with a good knowledge of the immediate area. Having a bright and friendly personality is an asset. Most of the work is of the counter variety though some officers occasionally may be expected to show visiting agents, press or VIPs around.

How can you Work for a Tourist Office?

There simply is no precise way or guaranteed training that will get you a position with a tourist board or information centre. It really is as much a question of luck as of judgement. An English or other language degree, a marketing degree, or writing ability can be extremely useful if you have aspirations to reach the top, but do not dismiss the backdoor route of office work, accountancy or personnel.

The City and Guilds have designed courses in tourism which lead to a COTICC certificate of competence for tourist information staff, but you need a job first before you can take this part-time programme.

Other Opportunities

Every tourist attraction needs people to promote it, write about it, market it and show people around. The range is a very wide one, from historic houses and museums to marinas, recreational areas and safari parks. A museum curator or assistant almost undoubtedly needs specialised experience, for example a study of history, sociology, archaeology, etc. But, for those out to market it, a sales background is preferable.

The Tourist Guide

Unfortunately, it is not so easy to be a tourist guide as you might anticipate. It is not just a question of knowing your home town well, but one of age and competing with a host of hopefuls to get accepted on a training course that leads to a 'blue badge' guide qualification.

Regional tourist boards (including the London Tourist Board) run courses of varying lengths but there are always hundreds of applicants. The London Tourist Board, for example, runs an annual part-time course for 35 candidates over a six-month period. You must first fill in an application form, then attend a pre-interview test on general knowledge relevant to guiding. If you are successful at that, you will then be called for an interview proper when you will be assessed mostly on personality, appearance and attitude. At the end of the course, there is a stiff written and practical exam which, when passed, gives the 'blue badge' nationally recognised qualification.

Although there are no specific educational requirements, tourist boards usually look for candidates in the 25 to 55 age bracket. Some areas, where the need for tourism is great, may accept younger people, or may run only a one- or two-week course. A working committee for regional tourist boards has drawn up a national standard of requirements for guiding which it hopes will eventually be accepted by all tourist boards. The Guild of Guide Lecturers, 2 Bridge Street, London SW1A 2JR; tel: 01-839 7438, is the professional body in this country for guiding and will pass along information on what courses are available although it does not run them itself.

The Tour Manager

Guides who escort a tour (tour managers) are generally self-employed. Of possible benefit here is application for membership to the International Association of Tour Managers, 397 Walworth Road, London SE17; tel: 01-703 9154. Qualifications for 'silver badge' membership are at least three years of international experience, working at least 60 days a year; and for 'gold badge', five years.

Chapter 6
Cruise Lines

Working on a ship could prove a fascinating experience; it could take you to far corners of the globe, or act as interim work experience before you finally settle on a career. Although cruise ships try to employ nationals wherever possible, foreign passenger lines do require some British staff if they are selling to the British travelling public.

Career Opportunities

Administrative work for a shipping line includes: office duties; sales and marketing; press and public relations; and reservations. On the operational side, the main jobs are for caterers, stewards and pursers. Entertainers are in constant demand and, of course, ships do have their own medical and engineering teams. Large cruise liners require hairdressers, sales people for their shops and boutiques, and croupiers when they have a casino on board.

The advantages of working at sea are obvious, but do remember the disadvantages: stewards and pursers may have to work seven days a week with little free time; hairdressers and sales staff (unlike officers, entertainers and social hostesses) do not mix with the passengers; space is restricted and the wrong type of person stuck on board for weeks at a time (like one young hairdresser told us) could go 'stir crazy'.

The Steward

Stewards might work on a passenger or cargo ship. On the former, his/her tasks tend to be specialised, such as serving in the restaurant or working in the pantry or stores. On the latter, a steward could well be expected to clean, make beds, etc, besides serving meals.

Basic catering training (for young men only) is given at the National Sea Training College, Gravesend, but any catering training is worthwhile before going to sea.

All catering personnel must be registered with the Merchant Navy Establishment Administration and be members of the National Union of Seamen. A shipping company is able to recommend waiters and bar stewards for membership if they have either at least 18 months' experience in a hotel or restaurant and/or have successfully completed the City and Guilds of London Institute exam in general catering.

Promotion is generally from within, so that a waiter could move on to become section waiter, assistant head waiter and head waiter. Alternatively, promotion might lead to public room steward, assistant barman, public room barman and bar services manager. Or you might be considered as a bedroom steward, which leads to assistant accommodation supervisor, then accommodation supervisor.

A cruise line will provide food and accommodation for free and will usually grant ten days' leave per month served on board, but you will be expected to pay for your own uniform. The minimum age is 20.

Kitchen Staff

A cruise line chef is responsible for a great deal of food preparation for a great number of people. With an eye to this career, you would be starting as a number three cook, butcher or baker with a company like P & O. Qualifications for third cook are City and Guilds passes 706/1 and 706/2 and some practical experience in a top class establishment. The minimum age is 20.

Your duties might involve the preparation and cooking of fish or grills, or you may be the stove cook. You may be requested to assist the larder cooks or be given the position of crew pantryman.

As a third baker, you will need: City and Guilds in bakery; catering college training in all aspects of baking; or completion of an apprenticeship as a baker. Duties might involve assistance with the preparation of sweets; the making of breads; or in the dairy section.

As a third butcher, you must have first served apprenticeship in a meat and poultry establishment. Work will involve dissecting and preparing joints and cuts of all types of meat plus freezer work.

In all cases, food and accommodation are free but you have to provide standard working clothes.

The Purser

The purser is head of what, these days, cruise ships call 'hotel services afloat', and is responsible directly to the captain. It is a job that requires excellent organisational abilities plus diplomacy; helping passengers calls for patience, courtesy and tact. The purser's bureau answers questions and enquiries, cashes travellers cheques and deals with all the documentation and the crew work of the ship, so accounting and clerical skills are essential.

Initial recruitment is as junior assistant purser either for administration or for catering. Qualifications for the former are secretarial skills - 55 wpm typing and 120 wpm shorthand - reception and cash handling experience. Knowledge of a continental language is an advantage. Entry to the catering side demands graduate membership of the Hotel Catering and Institutional Management Association, or the Higher National Diploma in hotelkeeping and catering operations, plus a minimum of one year's full-time practical experience.

Applicants must be aged between 21 and 26 and will be requested to attend a preliminary interview, a selection board and pass a medical before acceptance.

Promotion leads to the title of assistant purser whose duties are similar with added responsibilities. From there the ladder is to senior assistant purser and then to deputy purser. The deputies take care of victualling, service to passengers and control of the crew. The deputy purser (catering) oversees the chef's side of things (kitchen organisation, preparation and cooking of food, ship's storerooms), while the deputy purser (accommodation) looks after the passengers' cabin service, dining and other public rooms.

Junior assistant pursers earn paid leave at around 229 days per service year. During their first six months at sea they will be assessed, after which there is an interview and review of career prospects. Officers in the purser's department are expected to pay for their own uniforms.

Deck and Engineer Officers

An approach to these careers is to start as a cadet and receive as much sea-going training as possible on a variety of vessels before being selected to join the passenger division. A shipping company will probably suggest cadet application if you are between 16 and 18 years and have six O levels including maths, English language and physics (or mechanics, physics with chemistry, or engineering science).

Radio Officers

To think in this direction, you will first have to have gained the Ministry of Post and Telecommunications General Certificate in Marine Radio-communications, and a Department of Trade and Industry Radar Maintenance Certificate.

Electrical Officers

Entrants need a T4 ONC or HNC qualification or equivalent, and a suitable apprenticeship to become an assistant electrical officer. Promotion leads to second electrical officer, first electrical officer and senior first electrical officer. Duties are primarily concerned with the operation, maintenance and voyage repairs of all electrical equipment installed.

Other Possibilities

A registered general nurse with a registered midwife certificate could find work on board a cruise ship. A qualified infant or junior school teacher might find a position as a children's hostess. Printers, telephonists and cinema projectionists are also called for.

Chapter 7
Other UK Holiday Operations

When it comes to looking at careers in travel and the holiday industry, it is clear that there are many opportunities. A degree in archaeology, economics, sociology, etc, is no set-back to what may later become travel work. Tourism, after all, is to do with leisure.

Working in the leisure industry can mean involvement with tourist attractions, wildlife parks, gardens and a host of other interesting jobs. When it comes to courses you could take to help you on your way, leisure – like tourism itself – is a relatively new component. BTEC, for example, has approved courses that lead not only to a business qualification with recreation options, but to the new leisure studies award. Those already working full-time in the recreational area may take courses run by the Institute of Baths and Recreational Management, on a day-release basis at seven colleges, while the City and Guilds has developed a course for operational staff in visitor attractions to be made available in selected areas. The Institute of Amenity Management has introduced a Certificate and Diploma qualification and there are also degree courses in leisure and recreation at an increasing number of higher education centres.

Boating Holidays

A boating holiday does not necessarily mean cruise ship work. If you have ever taken a boating holiday in England, you will realise there is a wider range. Britain has over 2,000 miles of waterways: the Midlands, for example, has more miles of canals than Venice, while the favourite stretches continue to be the Norfolk Broads, the Thames, the Avon and the Scottish waterways.

Blakes is one of the leading operators in this holiday field having started in 1908. Basically, this is a managing company which acts as agent for around 100 independent boat hire companies. Some are small family-owned businesses; others are much larger with a limitless choice of boats. As managing agent, Blakes sets the standards (every boat must comply with these), produces a brochure and takes the bookings. The company, therefore, has its own managing director and marketing team, representatives and reservations. A public relations agency tells the company's message. Like every operator or agent worth their salt, Blakes continually looks to expand its programme. For example, in 1984 they introduced international boating holidays that included the rivers and loughs of Ireland, French and Dutch waterways, and flotilla sailing in Greece and Yugoslavia.

Blakes has to cost and negotiate with boatyards and owners so people with an accountancy background are needed. Since it is a direct-book firm, it operates a telephone booking service seven days a week.

Hoseasons (another well-known agent for boating companies) distributes its brochures via Martins the Newsagent and other travel agencies, as well as keepng its traditional direct-sell aspect. A company marketing exercise in 1984 meant that additional brochures were promoted in 200 selected post offices and that the public could choose their holiday from Littlewoods stores all over the UK.

Innovative ideas are a must in the travel industry. Hoseasons, for instance, expanded into holiday homes, first on a self-catering level and then with meal-inclusive programmes at eight holiday centres providing daytime activities and evening entertainment. The company introduced the term 'country club centres', which are self-catering homes based around a manor or castle where country club style facilities are available.

There are also jobs relating more directly to boating; one could be called upon to skipper or crew a boat, for example. Sailing enthusiasts might put their hobby to profitable use, become flotilla leaders or part of the team. Basic catering knowledge is useful for boating holidays where everything is done for the passenger. Further expansion of thought brings in the watersport centres – sailing instruction, maintenance, starting up a windsurfing school, etc.

Holiday Centres

Butlins, Pontins, etc, no longer call themselves holiday camps, but holiday or leisure centres. What they provide is a totally inclusive programme with a schedule of activities, events and entertainment. On the in-house side, they must market, sell and promote. On-site, they must manage, cater, and look after the holiday-makers. A nursing or child-care background could be beneficial; experience as a sport instructor is also useful. Other areas of work include kitchen and bar staff, and food and beverage control. The ability to organise and an outgoing personality are assets for the job of 'Redcoat' or entertainer.

A teaching background does not limit you to work in schools. These days, speciality interest/training is needed for hotel and holiday centre vacations. Activity courses are very popular on the holiday scene, whether it be photography, flower arranging, riding, painting or computer knowledge.

Health Clubs

Health is such a 1980s state of mind that it has turned into a profitable industry of its own. But health clubs do not always have to be severely medical – they, too, are geared to relaxation and leisure. A beauty or nutritional training could lead to a job with an independent health club – they are scattered all over the country, but are especially predominant in London. It could also lead to a job in a hotel health club. Practically every new hotel being built has its own health centre with pool, jacuzzi, sauna, steam rooms, gym and massage rooms. Even the older established hotels (such as the Metropole in Brighton) have added these facilities and require personnel with expertise to run and work in them. Courses are also being run in hotels abroad, so here again the scope is boundless.

Stately Homes

There is no consortium *per se* of stately homes where the general public may book holidays, but several of our British stately homes do, in fact, either accept weekend guests as their guests (ie, they act as hosts), or hire out their homes for a week or more. Prices are naturally in accordance with the accommodation and prestige being offered.

Since the upkeep of stately homes is extremely expensive, the larger estates are often compelled to think of ways of paying for that upkeep. In many cases, that may mean tours around part of a home. It may mean that an amusement park or recreational area of some kind will be added to the estate to encourage the public to spend money. In other instances, a hotel or tour rep will sell a 'guest of a lord' them to overseas visitors on a commissionable basis. In each of these cases, there is a need for staff to serve tea, to act as informed guides, and to manage the actual property, bearing in mind fishing and hunting rights, etc. A training in horticulture could result in a position with a stately home's estate – an end result you might not have anticipated.

Bed and Breakfast

Frankly, anyone can run a bed and breakfast guest house, if they can run a home. If you can make a couple of beds, cook bacon and eggs and dust a living room, you could start your own business. Making that business profitable, however, is another story. Being in the right location has a lot to do with success. Registering with the local tourist board gives authenticity, but it also means extra rates. There is no corsortium of bed and breakfast guest houses but publications are available, listing accredited ones throughout the country.

Country House Hotels

This term usually refers not only to a rural location but to a type of operation: small, intimate and with the atmosphere of a private home. These need not be expensive but some, with special emphasis on personal service and style, ask the same rates as large city hotels. Unlike the latter, though, the small country hotels tend to hire young local people for their staff, preferring to train them to their own particular requirements, rather than affording the salary of a management trainee who could be set in a chain hotel mould.

Coaching Companies

Coaching operations involve much more than driving large vehicles. National Express, for example, operates a vast network throughout the UK and abroad. Within the organisation there are many levels of tour and travel work calling for a variety of knowledge.

Such companies are often divided into subsidiaries dealing with different market segments. Besides travel from A to B, there may be tour movement sectors, conference traffic, city sightseeing and maybe an executive hire section when on-board hostesses are in demand.

Rail Travel

Working for the railways does not only mean being a train driver, guard or ticket collector. The Railways Board, like the tourist boards and airlines, covers a wide gamut of jobs. It, too, has its planning and research divisions, its conference office, its sales and marketing department, and its press and promotions office. Equally, you could work in reservations and ticketing or even in catering as a cook or a steward.

British Rail has its own management trainee schemes. Candidates can be either graduates or clerical staff. Although the majority of business is naturally associated with transport, British Rail is involved in other fields, such as engineering manufacture, shipping, catering, consultancy and working with continental railways. The prime asset you could possess for entering management is the ability to communicate with people at all levels. Graduates opting for the passenger business section must have a flair for identifying new opportunities in the travel market and an interest in using analytical and numerate skills to design and develop services. Training for the freight businesses involves: the determining of individual needs of industries, manufacturers and distributors; planning the logistics; negotiating the price; and making sure the contracts work and pay.

Passenger and freight divisions both come under business management, but there are other career areas, namely: operations management; finance/accountancy management; personnel management; engineering management; engineering and scientific research and development; operational research; computer programming; quantity surveying; estate management; and catering management.

To apply for one of the training schemes you should have, or expect to have, an honours degree. Some additional requirements apply to certain schemes but if you want further information, your careers office will put you in touch with the local BritRail contract officer.

Case Study

Gary joined BritRail straight from school and was trained on the spot as a steward.

> You don't need any qualifications but good English is an obvious help, as is appearance – you are, after all, in close contact with passengers. My head steward trained me but there is a restaurant car which has

been turned into a special training school, which travels up and down the country. Courses are given on this at the various stops it makes.

I work three days a week though they vary and I never know which train I'll be on or where I'll be going on what is known as my 'spare' day. The rest of the time, I stick to the same route. For me that means four trips a day, taking about 14½ hours - a typical day for most stewards. There are three stewards and one stewardess on my train, all working as a team under a head steward. The trays of food are heavy so you need to be fairly strong and serving food on a fast moving train has its problems!

On each of the four trips we serve breakfast, lunch, high tea and dinner. We also lay up and clear away and wash up. I sometimes do special work on exhibition trains or VIP excursions. The perks include tips from customers and also free rail passes and reduced fares.

Chapter 8
Business Travel

What is Business Travel?

The answer is precisely what it says – travel arrangements for anyone visiting a destination in a business capacity as opposed to a holiday one. Hence an airline's 'business class' (though it may use another name like 'club' or 'ambassador', etc) is geared to a frequent traveller who needs that extra amount of leg room and slightly better service because flying itself is merely part of the day's work. Hence, also, the 'business hotel' which is liable to offer amenities necessary to the guest who may not have scheduled or social hours, such as 24-hour room service, mini bars, same day valet service, etc. Additionally, the business class hotel will have services like telex, secretarial, etc, automatically and will be able to offer varying sized function rooms for private meetings, conferences or meals.

Business travel may involve an individual or it may involve a group. Work in this segment of the travel industry may mean making the travel arrangements for many executives in a company totally unrelated to travel, or it may mean working in a travel agency specifically dealing with business group travel. It may mean arranging a conference for a company totally unrelated to travel; being a conference planner for several different companies; being a conference executive at a hotel, tourist board, city council, etc; or a sales executive for a conference centre.

Conference Travel

As mentioned above, this is part of the business travel scene as it relates to groups of people attending a meeting in this country or abroad. It is a growing part of the travel industry and well worth career consideration.

From the point of view of a hotel or other venue, a good selling technique is vital. Conference executives must promote their own venue as *the* right one for given groups to bring in the business. They will be expected to know their product thoroughly and only sell it to those for whom it is suitable, if they are hoping for repeat business. They will be expected to negotiate rates that are profitable to their own venue and appropriate to the buyers. Inevitably they will be called upon to make sales calls which may mean travelling abroad as well as throughout the UK.

The conference organiser on the other hand has a buying job. He/she must be sure enough of a company's requisites to give an exact brief to a planner, agent, hotel or conference centre. So far, there are few really professional organisers with enough expertise to negotiate their own packages. Quite often, a company will ask almost any member of staff to arrange their annual meeting, function, outing, etc.

A conference planner is somebody who will have had a varied experience in the travel industry. Like a tour operator, the planner should be able to package various elements, suggest suitable destinations and venues, and create interesting ideas for social programmes and events.

A conference officer is likely to work for a city or town council 'selling' the place as a whole rather than a particular venue within it. He/she has a thorough knowledge of what is available in the area, for whom and for what numbers it would be suitable and why. Conference enquiries and sometimes also bookings are handled.

Incentive Travel

Incentive trips are what companies offer their personnel as a reward for increased business. Sales teams are often the target – those selling over and above certain amounts being eligible for the holiday. In order to make employees desirous of doing better to gain the trip, the trip itself has to be of an exciting nature.

There are growing numbers of travel companies specialising entirely in incentive travel arrangements. Here again, it is packaging various holiday elements, but generally not on a cut-price basis. An incentive organiser is expected to be creative and imaginative. Theme parties, unusual venues, and out-of-the-ordinary things to do become necessities: the right hotel with the same accommodation and treatment for all winners; the right mode of travel to inspire greater work efforts; and an itinerary that sounds appealing.

Chapter 9
Public Relations, Press and Promotion Work

In one word, this is communications. Almost every aspect of the travel world has a person or department dealing with the media to publicise and market destination, product, image or event. There is no guaranteed route to a career in these areas but for details of available courses that could benefit pursuers of this sector of the travel industry, see Part 2.

The Travel PRO
The travel public relations officer may work in-house for a tour company or for a public relations agency that handles that account. Skills required to become a travel PRO are the same for most other areas of public relations: a talent for writing, as press releases will be part of the job; a flair for organisation to cope with events, promotions and brochure launches that relate to the client; and the right likeable attitude for working with other people, particularly those in the media.

Creativity – a flow of ideas – is an important aspect of the job. Knowledge of print, layout and production costs is often helpful. A journalistic background regularly leads to a position in public relations and any course in marketing or communications could well earn you an executive opening.

Courses in both the aforementioned subjects are available from diploma to degree level but, if you want to start young and learn the practical way, take the secretarial route.

Case Studies
Sarah currently works as a travel account executive in a consultant public relations firm. Now in her 20s, she left school to take a post-A level, two-year bilingual secretarial course.

> The language really helped. When I'd completed the course I went off

to Paris and was offered a copywriting job with an ad agency. When I returned to England, I worked as a personal assistant in a PR consultancy and then, by luck, as deputy editor of a travel magazine.

Sarah agrees that the 'rounded out' experience was what got her a job with her current employer, first as an assistant account executive and now as a senior one. What does her present job comprise?

> Running the account on a day-to-day level is a mainstay, by keeping constant liaison with the client and the press. There's a constant need to generate ideas, both for the client's own promotions and the writers' story angles. Naturally there are news and feature releases to be written and press trips to be organised, co-ordinated and often escorted. Functions and press parties have to be set up and the job may call for the ability to negotiate print and art costs.

The salary range for a public relations officer is an exceptionally broad one. At its most senior level it can run to £20,000 pa or, indeed, much much more. At its junior level, it is more likely to be £8,000 to £9,000 pa.

Eugene, also in her 20s, is also a PR agency employee and equally, to get there, she travelled the secretarial way.

> I taught myself copy typing but it was my second employer who sent me to secretarial school. I wanted to work in PR but it's really a matter of timing to find – and get – the right vacancy. When I did, I joined a consultancy as a secretary-cum-assistant to a travel account executive which meant I learnt all there was to know on the job. When the account executive left, I had to step in to hold the fort, proved I could do it, and now I'm fully fledged.

Eugene's work is pretty similar to Sarah's but she adds:

> The travel PRO may well have to attend several annual conventions as a client representative; hire guest speakers or entertainers for certain functions; assist with audiovisual presentations; come up with giveaway possibilities and follow through on obtaining and distributing them.

The Travel Writer

There is no set way to become a travel writer. The system which applies to fashion, feature or news writing will similarly apply to the travel field but, because it is considered to be one of the most glamorous areas with some of the best perks, it is also one of the most competitive to break into. When such an opening occurs on a newspaper or magazine, it is often offered to another existing member of staff covering a completely different area. On the other hand, a secretarial position could eventually lead to it as might freelance writing.

If you want to ensure a career in journalism (of any kind), it is best to apply to a local or regional paper for employment as an indentured trainee. If you pass the probationary period, you will be sent on block-release to a college accredited by the National Council for the Training of Journalists (NCTJ). You could also apply direct to the latter for a place on the one-year full-time, pre-entry course, or in some cases receive training on the spot from newspaper groups whose schemes meet the NCTJ requirements.

With natural writing talent and a bit of a pushy streak, you could be lucky enough to omit all this, by beavering away at trying to sell articles until you get one published. If the disappointment of several rejections is too much, then a writing career is not for you, but if you study the market for which you wish to write first, can type clean copy to style, either amusing or factual, you stand a chance.

Case Study

Andy (23) did not have training, but he did like to write. After a couple of years getting nowhere, he acquired a freelance contract to write travel for a giveaway magazine. Though it subsequently folded, he is now the travel editor for a prestigious national glossy magazine.

> It took a lot of knocking on doors, futile effort and time and many disappointments. But, finally, I found an editor who liked the way I wrote and I was called in for an interview. Once you have published articles to show, you're on your way to becoming a name.

Young hopefuls will not be able to join the Guild of British Travel Writers until they can prove they have been published or have been hired by a reputable publication, radio or TV station, and earn the majority of their income from travel writing.

The Travel Photographer

The British Institute of Professional Photography recognises several courses that are available but, if you have an eye for the visual, a City and Guilds qualification in general photography might start you off. An inherent knack for taking a good picture is the alternative.

Most travel photographers have covered other fields before they specialise in this area. Aspects different from studio work include lenses used (eg, a wide angle is a must for shooting hotel bedrooms/bathrooms); natural lighting (eg, when the light falls just right on some well known landmark); a blue sky (for selling summer sun pictures to travel brochures); and a 'feel' for the market to know what kind of photographs do sell.

The best way to make money is to establish a photo library and a list of repeat tour operator clients, and acquire an agent.

Part 2

Chapter 10
Courses and Training

Key to Abbreviations

BTEC	Business and Technician Education Council
C	College
CAD	College of Art and Design
CAg	College of Agriculture
CAT	College of Art and Technology
CCom	College of Commerce
CD&T	College of Design and Technology
CF&HE	College of Further and Higher Education
CFE	College of Further Education
CFEA&D	College of Further Education, Art and Design
CGLI	City and Guilds of London Institute
CHE	College of Higher Education
CH & FE	College of Higher and Further Education
CNAA	Council for National Academic Awards
COTAC	Certificate of Travel Agency Competence
CT	College of Technology
CTA	College of Technology and Agriculture
CT & D	College of Technology and Design
Dip	Diploma
HND	Higher National Diploma
IHE	Institute of Higher Education
LCCI	London Chamber of Commerce and Industry
Met C	Metropolitan College
Poly	Polytechnic
SAcc	School of Accounting
SchIns	School of Insurance
SCOTVEC	Scottish Vocational Education Council
SHND	Scottish Higher National Diploma
SNC	Scottish National Certificate
TC	Technical College
TC & SA	Technical College and School of Art

Diploma and Certificate Courses

Courses in Travel and Tourism
Aberdeen CCom: SCOTVEC National Cert Tourism, HND in Business Studies (Travel & Tourism), COTAC 1 & 2
Amersham CFEA & D: BTEC National Dip Business & Finance (Travel & Tourism), COTAC 1 & 2, COTAM
Aylesbury C: BTEC National Dip Business & Finance (Travel & Tourism), CGLI Travel Studies
Barking CT: BTEC National Dip Business & Finance (Travel & Tourism)
Barry CFE: BTEC National Dip Business Studies (Travel & Tourism)
Bell CT (Hamilton): SCOTVEC HND Business Studies (Travel & Tourism)
Birmingham C of Food and Domestic Arts: BTEC National Cert Business & Finance (Travel & Tourism)
Bishop Burton CAg: BTEC National Dip Business and Finance (Rural Tourism). College Dip Business & Rural Tourism
Bournemouth & Poole CFE: BTEC National Dip Business and Finance (Travel & Tourism); College award Cert in Travel Agency Practice; College Dip Travel and Tourism
Braintree CFE: BTEC National Dip Business Studies (Travel & Tourism), CGLI Travel Studies
Bridgend CT: BTEC National Dip Business & Finance (Travel & Tourism)
Brighton CT BTEC National Dip Business & Finance (Travel & Tourism); BTEC National Dip Travel & Tourism
Bristol Poly: BTEC HND Business & Finance, Tourism specialism.
Brooklands TC: BTEC National Dip Business & Finance
Broxtowe CFE (Nottingham): BTEC National Dip Business & Finance (Travel & Tourism), COTAC 1 & 2
Brunel TC (Bristol): Tourist Guide's cert
Bury MetC: BTEC National Dip Business Studies (Travel & Tourism)
Cambridge CFE: BTEC National Dip Business & Finance (Travel & Tourism); BTEC National Dip Distribution Studies (Travel & Tourism, Leisure Studies)
Carlisle TC: BTEC National Dip Business Studies (Travel & Tourism)
Carmarthenshire CTA: Cert Farm Tourism
Carshalton CFE: BTEC National Dip Business & Finance (Travel & Tourism) COTAC 1 & 2; CGLI Cert Travel Studies
Central CCom (Glasgow): SCOTVEC National Cert modules travel and tourism; SCOTVEC HNC Business Studies (Travel & Tourism)
Central Manchester C: BTEC National Dip Business & Finance (Travel & Tourism); COTAC 1 & 2
Craven C (Skipton): COTAC 1
Crosskeys Tertiary C: BTEC National Dip Business & Finance (Travel & Tourism)

de Havilland C: BTEC National Cert Business & Finance (Travel & Tourism); COTAC 1 & 2
Derby CFE: BTEC National Dip Business & Finance (Travel & Tourism); COTAC 1
Distributive Trades C: BTEC National Dip Business & Finance (Travel & Tourism), HND Business & Finance (Travel & Tourism); COTAC 1; COTAM
Dorset IHE: BTEC HND Business & Finance, Tourism specialism
Dudley CT: BTEC National Dip Business & Finance (Travel & Tourism); COTAC 1
Dumfries & Galloway CT: SCOTVEC HND Business Studies (Travel & Tourism)
Dundee CCom: SCOTVEC National Cert modules, travel & tourism; SCOTVEC HND Business Studies (Travel & Tourism); COTAC 1
Ealing CHE: BTEC HND Business & Finance, Travel & Tourism specialism
Eastbourne CAT: BTEC National Dip Business & Finance (Travel & Tourism); College Award Travel Personnel Dip; British Airways Ticketing course
East Devon CFE: College Dip Tourism
Eastleigh CFE: BTEC National Dip Business & Finance (Travel & Tourism)
East Surrey C (Redhill): BTEC National Dip Business Studies (Travel & Tourism); CGLI Travel Studies; College Dip Travel & Tourism; COTAC 1
Erith CT: BTEC National Dip Business Studies (Travel & Tourism); CGLI Travel Studies
Falkirk CT: SCOTVEC National Cert modules, Travel & Tourism;
Farnborough CT: BTEC National Dip Business & Finance (Travel & Tourism); HND Business & Finance, Tourism Specialism; COTAC 1 & 2
Garretts Green C (Birmingham): BTEC National Dip Business & Finance (Travel & Tourism); COTAC 1
Glasgow C of Food Technology: SCOTVEC National Cert modules, Travel & Tourism; SCOTVEC HNC Business Studies (Travel & Tourism); SCOTVEC HND Business Studies (Travel & Tourism); COTAC 1
Grantham CFE: BTEC National Dip Business & Finance (Travel & Tourism)
Halesowen C: BTEC National Dip Business & Finance (Travel & Tourism)
Handsworth TC: COTAC 1 & 2
Hendon CFE: BTEC National Dip Business & Finance (Travel & Tourism)
Henley C (Coventry): BTEC National Dip Business & Finance (Travel & Tourism); CGLI Travel Studies; COTAC 1 & 2; College Cert Travel Agency Practice; British Airways Fares & Ticketing 1 & 2

Highbury CT (Portsmouth): BTEC National Dip Business & Finance (Travel & Tourism); COTAC 1 & 2

High Peak CFE (Buxton): BTEC National Dip Business & Finance (Travel & Tourism); COTAC 1

Huddersfield TC: COTAC 1 & 2; COTAM

Isle of Wight CAT: COTAC 1

Kendal CFE: BTEC National Dip Business & Finance (Travel & Tourism)

Lancaster & Morecambe CFE: BTEC National Dip Business Studies (Travel & Tourism); CGLI Cert Travel Studies

Langley C: BTEC National Cert Business & Finance (Travel & Tourism); National Dip Business & Finance (Travel & Tourism)

Lewes TC: BTEC National Dip Business & Finance (Travel & Tourism); COTAC 1

Lincoln CT: BTEC National Dip Business & Finance (Travel & Tourism)

London International C: COTAC 1 & 2; College Dip Travel & Tourism

Loughborough TC: BTEC National Dip Business & Finance (Travel & Tourism); COTAC 1; College Dip Travel & Tourism; British Airways Ticketing course

Lowestoft CFE: BTEC National Dip Business & Finance (Travel & Tourism)

Macclesfield CFE: BTEC National Dip Business Studies

Mid-Cornwall CFE: BTEC National Dip Business Studies (Travel & Tourism)

Motherwell C: SCOTVEC National Cert modules, travel & tourism

Napier C (Edinburgh): SCOTVEC HND Business Studies (Travel & Tourism)

Newbury CFE: BTEC National Dip Business & Finance (Travel & Tourism)

New C (Durham): BTEC National Dip Business & Finance (Travel & Tourism); HND Business & Finance, Travel and Tourism specialism; BTEC HND Business Studies (Tourism Management); BTEC HND Business Studies (Leisure Administration); COTAC 1 & 2; COTAM; College Cert Travel & Tourism

Newcastle CAT: COTAC 1 & 2

Newcastle Poly: BTEC HND Business & Finance, Travel & Tourism specialism

Norfolk CAT: BTEC National Dip Business Studies (Travel & Tourism)

Northbrook CD&T (Chichester): BTEC National Dip Business Studies (Travel & Tourism); HND Business & Finance, Travel & Tourism specialism; COTAC 1

North Lindsey CT: BTEC National Dip Business & Finance (Travel & Tourism)

North Nottinghamshire CFE: BTEC National Cert Business & Finance (Travel & Tourism)

North Tyneside CFE: BTEC National Dip Business Studies (Travel & Tourism)

North West Kent CT: BTEC National Dip Business & Finance (Travel & Tourism)
Norwich City CF&HE: BTEC National Dip Business & Finance (Travel & Tourism)
Paddington C: BTEC National Dip Business Studies (Travel & Tourism); CGLI Travel Studies
Park Lane CFE (Leeds): COTAC 1 & 2: COTAM; British Airways ticketing course
Percival Whitley CFE (Halifax): BTEC National Dip Business & Finance (Travel & Tourism)
Peterborough Regional C: BTEC National Dip Business & Finance (Travel & Tourism)
Plymouth CFE: COTAC 1 & 2
Plymouth Poly: BTEC HND Business & Finance, Travel & Tourism specialism
Pontypridd TC: National Cert Business & Finance (Travel & Tourism)
Redditch C: BTEC National Cert Business & Finance (Travel & Tourism); National Dip Business & Finance (Travel & Tourism); COTAC 1 & 2
Rockingham CFE: BTEC National Dip Business & Finance (Travel & Tourism); COTAC 1
Rupert Stanley CFE (Belfast): BTEC National Dip Business Studies (Travel & Tourism)
St Helens C: BTEC National Dip Business & Finance (Travel & Tourism); COTAC 1 & 2
Salisbury CT: COTAC 1 & 2
Solihull CT: BTEC National Cert Business & Finance (Travel & Tourism); COTAC 1 & 2; COTAM
Somerset CAT: COTAC 1, Basic Tourist Guide course, Rural Tourism
Soundwell TC: BTEC National Dip Business & Finance (Travel & Tourism); COTAC 1
Southall CT: BTEC National Dip Business & Finance (Travel & Tourism)
South Bristol TC: BTEC National Dip Business & Finance (Travel & Tourism)
South Cheshire C: BTEC National Dip Business Studies (Travel & Tourism); COTAC 1
South Downs CFE (Havant): COTAC 1
South Glamorgan IHE: BTEC HND Business & Finance, Tourism specialism
South Kent CT: BTEC National Dip Business & Finance (Travel & Tourism)
Southport CAT: BTEC National Dip Business & Finance (Travel & Tourism); COTAC 1 & 2; CGLI Travel Studies
Southwark C: BTEC National Dip Business & Finance (Travel & Tourism); COTAC 1
South Warwickshire CFE: CGLI Travel Studies

Stannington C (Sheffield): BTEC National Dip Business & Finance (Travel & Tourism); COTAC 1
Stockport CT: BTEC HND Business & Finance, Travel & Tourism specialism
Tamworth CFE: BTEC National Dip Business & Finance (Travel & Tourism)
Telford CFE (Edinburgh): SCOTVEC National Cert modules, travel & tourism
Thurrock TC: College Dip Travel & Tourism
Trent Poly: BTEC HND Business Studies (Tourism)
Tresham C (Kettering & Corby): BTEC National Dip Business & Finance (Travel & Tourism); CGLI Travel Studies
Trowbridge TC: BTEC National Dip Business & Finance (Travel & Tourism)
Waltham Forest C: BTEC National Dip Business & Finance (Travel & Tourism)
West Glamorgan IHE: BTEC HND Business & Finance, Travel & Tourism specialism
West Kent CFE: BTEC National Dip Business & Finance (Travel & Tourism); COTAC 1
Windsor & Maidenhead C: COTAC 1
Worcester TC: BTEC National Dip Business & Finance (Travel & Tourism); College Tourist Guides course.

Courses in Catering and Hotel Management
Blackpool and Fylde C: BTEC HND Hotel and Catering Management
Dorset IHE: BTEC Higher Dip, Hotel Catering and Institutional Management
Highbury CT (Portsmouth): BTEC HND Hotel Catering and Institutional Management
Llandrillo TC: BTEC HND Hotel and Catering Management
Leeds Poly: BTEC HND Hotel Catering and Institutional Management
Manchester Poly: BTEC HND Hotel Catering and Institutional Management
Middlesex Poly: BTEC HND Hotel Catering and Institutional Management
North London Poly: BTEC HND Catering and Institutional Management
Robert Gordon's Institute of Technology, Aberdeen: SCOTVEC Higher Diploma in Hotel Catering and Institutional Management
Sheffield Poly: BTEC HND Hotel Catering and Institutional Management
Trent Poly: HND Hotel Catering and Institutional Management
Ulster Poly: DipHE Hotel and Catering Management; BTEC HND Hotel and Catering Management

Courses in Public Relations

Aberdeen CCom: SCOTVEC SHND Communication Studies, full-time
Airedale & Wharfedale CFE: CGLI 732 Communication Skills, level 1, day-release and evenings
Angus TC: CGLI 732 Communication Skills, level 1, day-release
Anniesland C, Glasgow: CGLI 732 Communication Skills, level 1, block-release and day-release
Ballymena TC: CGLI 732 Communication Skills, level 1, day-release
Basingstoke TC: LCCI Public Relations Certificate, full-time; CGLI 732 Communication Skills, level 1, day-release; CGLI Communication Skills, level 2, full-time and day-release
Bell CT, Hamilton: SCOTVEC SHND Communication Studies, full-time
Birmingham Poly: College Award, Dip in Communication Studies, full-time
Cardonald C, Glasgow: LCCI Public Relations Certificate, full-time; CGLI 732 Communication Skills, level 1, day-release
Central CCom, Glasgow: College Award, Certificate in Creative Communication, full-time
Clarendon CFE, Nottingham: LCCI Public Relations Certificate, full-time
Coatbridge C: CGLI 732 Communication Skills, level 1, day-release
College for the Distributive Trades, London: LCCI Public Relations Certificate, day-release and evenings
Duncraig Castle C, Plockton: LCCI Public Relations Certificate, full-time
Dundee CCom: SCOTVEC SHND Communication Studies, full-time
Eastbourne CFE: LCCI Public Relations Certificate, full-time
East Hertfordshire C: LCCI Public Relations Certificate, full-time
Elmwood Agricultural & TC, Cupar: LCCI Public Relations Certificate, full-time
Falkirk CT: SCOTVEC SHND Communication Studies, full-time; CGLI 732 Communication Skills, level 1, day-release
Fermanagh CFE: LCCI Public Relations Certificate, full-time; CGLI 732 Communication Skills, level 1, day-release; level 2, full-time and day-release
Glasgow C of Food Technology: LCCI Public Relations Certificate, full-time; CGLI 732 Communication Skills, level 1, day-release
Gloucestershire CAT: CGLI 732 Communication Skills, level 1, block-release; level 2, block-release
Granville C, Sheffield: CGLI 732 Communication Skills, level 1, day-release and evenings
Halesowen CFE: LCCI Public Relations Certificate, full-time; CGLI 732 Communication Skills, level 2, full-time
Hartlepool CFE: CGLI 732 Communication Skills, level 1, day-release
Hastings CAT: LCCI Public Relations Certificate, full-time
Hebburn TC: CGLI 732 Communication Skills, level 1, day-release

Herefordshire TC: LCCI Public Relations Certificate, full-time; CGLI 732 Communication Skills, level 1, day-release
Hull CFE: CGLI 732 Communication Skills, level 1, day-release
James Watt C, Greenock: CGLI 732 Communication Skills, level 1, day-release; level 2, day-release
Kirkcaldy CT: SCOTVEC SHND Communication Studies, full-time; CGLI 732 Communication Skills, level 1, day-release
Lews Castle C, Stornoway: CGLI 732 Communication Skills, level 1, day-release
Mabel Fletcher TC, Liverpool: LCCI Public Relations Certificate, full-time; CGLI 732 Communication Skills, level 1, block-release and day-release; level 2, full-time, block-release and day-release
Matthew Boulton TC, Birmingham: CGLI 732 Communication Skills, level 1, day-release; level 2, day-release
Merton TC: LCCI Public Relations Certificate, full-time; CGLI 732 Communication Skills, level 2, full-time
Mid-Gloucestershire TC: CGLI 732 Communication Skills, level 1, day-release; level 2, day-release
Moray CFE, Elgin: CGLI 732 Communication Skills, level 1, day-release
Napier Poly, Edinburgh: SCOTVEC SHND Communication Studies, full-time
New TC, Ballymoney: LCCI Public Relation Certificate, full-time
Newtownabbey TC: LCCI Public Relations Certificate, full-time; CGLI 732 Communication Skills, level 1, day-release; level 2, full-time
North Lindsey CT: CGLI 732 Communication Skills, level 1, day-release; level 2, day-release
Oswestry C: CGLI 732 Communication Skills, level 1, day-release; level 2, day-release
Peterborough TC: CGLI 732 Communication Skills, level 1, day-release; level 2, day-release
Redhill TC: College-based, Pre-vocational Media Studies, full-time
St Helens CT: LCCI Public Relations Certificate, full-time
Shirecliffe C, Sheffield: College Award, Dip in Media Studies, full-time
Somerset CAT: LCCI Public Relations Certificate, full-time; CGLI 732 Communication Skills, level 1, day-release; level 2, full-time and day-release
Southampton CHE: College Award, Dip in Creative Communication Studies, full-time
South Cheshire C: LCCI Public Relations Certificate, full-time; CGLI 732 Communication Skills, level 1, block-release and day-release; level 2, full-time, block-release and day-release
South Devon TC: CGLI 732 Communication Skills, level 1, block-release and day-release; level 2, block-release and day-release
South Gwent CFE: LCCI Public Relations Certificate, full-time: CGLI 732 Communication Skills, level 2, full-time
South Shields Management Training Centre: LCCI Public Relations Certificate, full-time

Springburn C, Glasgow: LCCI Public Relations Certificate, full-time; CGLI 732 Communication Skills, level 1, day-release
Telford CFE, Edinburgh: SCOTVEC SNC Media Studies, full-time
Weston-super-Mare TC & SA: LCCI Public Relations Certificate, full-time; CGLI 732 Communication Skills, level 1, day-release
Woolwich C: LCCI Public Relations Certificate, full-time

Courses in Marketing

Belfast CT: Institute of Marketing Qualifying Certificate Part 1, day-release and evenings: Institute of Marketing Qualifying Certificate Part 2; Institute of Marketing Dip in Marketing, full-time, day-release and evenings
Birmingham Poly: Institute of Marketing Dip in Marketing, evenings
Blackburn CT & D: Institute of Marketing Qualifying Certificate Part 1, day-release; Institute of Marketing Qualifying Certificate Part 2; Institute of Marketing Dip in Marketing, evenings; BTEC HND in Business Studies, marketing specialism, sandwich
Bolton IHE: BTEC HND Business Studies, marketing specialism, full-time
Bradford & Ilkley Community C: BTEC HND in Business Studies, marketing specialism, full-time and day-release
Bridgend CT: Institute of Marketing Qualifying Certificate Part 1, day-release; Institute of Marketing Qualifying Certificate Part 2
Bristol Poly: Institute of Marketing Dip in Marketing, evenings; BTEC HND Business Studies, marketing specialism, full-time
Brooklands TC: Institute of Marketing Qualifying Certificate Part 1, evenings; Institute of Marketing Qualifying Certificate Part 2
Buckinghamshire CHE: Institute of Marketing Qualifying Certificate Part 1, evenings; Institute of Marketing Qualifying Certificate Part 2; Institute of Marketing Dip in Marketing, evenings: BTEC HND in Business Studies, languages and marketing specialism, full-time and sandwich; BTEC HND Business Studies, marketing specialism, full-time and sandwich
Cambridgeshire CAT: BTEC HND Business Studies, marketing specialism, sandwich
Central CCom, Glasgow: Institute of Marketing Qualifying Certificate Part 1, day-release and evenings; Institute of Marketing Qualifying Certificate Part 2
City of London Poly: Institute of Marketing Qualifying Certificate Part 1, evenings; Institute of Marketing Qualifying Certificate Part 2; Institute of Marketing Dip in Marketing, evenings
College for the Distributive Trades, London: Institute of Marketing Qualifying Certificate Part 1, evenings; Institute of Marketing Qualifying Certificate Part 2; Institute of Marketing Dip in Marketing, day-release and evenings; BTEC HND Business Studies, market research specialism, full-time; BTEC HND Business Studies,

marketing specialism, full-time; LCCI Marketing Certificate, evenings; RSA Commerce (Marketing) Stage 3, evenings.

Cornwall TC: Institute of Marketing Qualifying Certificate Part 1, day-release and evenings; Institute of Marketing Qualifying Certificate Part 2

Crawley CT: Institute of Marketing Qualifying Certificate Part 1, evenings; Institute of Marketing Qualifying Certificate Part 2; BTEC HND Business Studies, marketing specialism, full-time and sandwich

Crewe & Alsager CHE: Institute of Marketing Dip in Marketing, evenings

Croydon C: Institute of Marketing Qualifying Certificate Part 1, evenings; Institute of Marketing Qualifying Certificate Part 2; Institute of Marketing Dip in Marketing, evenings; BTEC HND Business Studies, marketing specialism, full-time

Derbyshire CHE; BTEC HND Business Studies, marketing specialism, sandwich, day-release and evenings

Doncaster Metropolitan IHE: Institute of Marketing Qualifying Certificate Part 1, day-release; Institute of Marketing Qualifying Certificate Part 2

Dorset IHE: Institute of Marketing Qualifying Certificate Part 1, day-release; Institute of Marketing Qualifying Certificate Part 2; Institute of Marketing Dip in Marketing, day-release; BTEC HND Business Studies, marketing specialism, full-time

Dundee CCom: Institute of Marketing Qualifying Certificate Part 1, day-release and evenings; Institute of Marketing Qualifying Certificate Part 2; Institute of Marketing Dip in Marketing, day-release and evenings

Ealing CHE: Institute of Marketing Dip in Marketing, evenings; BTEC HND Business Studies, marketing specialism, full-time and sandwich

East Warwickshire CHE: Institute of Marketing Qualifying Certificate Part 1, day-release and evenings; Institute of Marketing Qualifying Certificate Part 2; Institute of Marketing Dip in Marketing, evenings

Falkirk CT: Institute of Marketing Qualifying Certificate Part 1, day-release and evenings; Institute of Marketing Qualifying Certificate Part 2

Farnborough CT: Institute of Marketing Qualifying Certificate Part 1, evenings; Institute of Marketing Qualifying Certificate Part 2; Institute of Marketing Dip in Marketing, evenings; BTEC HND Business Studies, marketing specialism, full-time and sandwich

Filton TC: Institute of Marketing Qualifying Certificate Part 1, evenings; Institute of Marketing Qualifying Certificate Part 2

Glasgow CT: Institute of Marketing Dip in Marketing, day-release and evenings

Gloucestershire CAT: Institute of Marketing Qualifying Certificate Part 1, evenings; Institute of Marketing Qualifying Certificate Part 2; Institute of Marketing Dip in Marketing, evenings

Grimsby CT: Institute of Marketing Qualifying Certificate Part 1, evenings; Institute of Marketing Qualifying Certificate Part 2

Gwent CHE: Institute of Marketing Qualifying Certificate Part 1, evenings; Institute of Marketing Qualifying Certificate Part 2; Institute of Marketing Dip in Marketing, evenings; BTEC HND Business Studies, marketing specialism, full-time

Hammersmith & West London C: BTEC HND Business Studies, marketing specialism, full-time

Harrow CHE: Institute of Marketing Dip in Marketing, evenings

Havering TC, Hornchurch: Institute of Marketing Qualifying Certificate Part 1, evenings; Institute of Marketing Qualifying Certificate Part 2

Highbury CT, Portsmouth: Institute of Marketing Qualifying Certificate Part 1, evenings; Institute of Marketing Qualifying Certificate Part 2

Huddersfield Poly: BTEC HND Business Studies, marketing specialism, full-time; College Award, Dip in Marketing full-time

Hull CHE: Institute of Marketing Dip in Marketing, evenings

Kidderminster CFE: Institute of Marketing Qualifying Certificate Part 1, block-release and day-release; Institute of Marketing Qualifying Certificate Part 2

Kirkby CFE: Institute of Marketing Qualifying Certificate Part 1, day-release and evenings; Institute of Marketing Qualifying Certificate Part 2

Kirkcaldy CT: Institute of Marketing Qualifying Certificate Part 1, day-release and evenings; Institute of Marketing Qualifying Certificate Part 2; Institute of Marketing Dip in Marketing, day-release and evenings

Leeds Poly: Institute of Marketing Dip in Marketing, evenings

Leicester Poly: Institute of Marketing Dip in Marketing, evenings

Liverpool Poly: Institute of Marketing Dip in Marketing, evenings

London SAcc: Institute of Marketing Qualifying Certificate Part 1, full-time, day-release and evenings; Institute of Marketing Qualifying Certificate Part 2; Institute of Marketing Dip in Marketing, full-time, day-release and evenings

London SchIns: Institute of Marketing Qualifying Certificate Part 1, full-time; Institute of Marketing Qualifying Certificate Part 2

Luton CHE: Institute of Marketing Qualifying Certificate Part 1, evenings; Institute of Marketing Qualifying Certificate Part 2; Institute of Marketing Dip in Marketing, evenings; BTEC HND Business Studies, marketing specialism, full-time and sandwich

Manchester Poly: Institute of Marketing Dip in Marketing, evenings

Matthew Boulton TC, Birmingham: Institute of Marketing Qualifying Certificate Part 1, evenings; Institute of Marketing Qualifying Certificate Part 2

Merton TC: Institute of Marketing Qualifying Certificate Part 1, evenings; Institute of Marketing Qualifying Certificate Part 2

Middlesex Poly: Institute of Marketing Dip in Marketing, evenings

Mid-Kent CH & FE: Institute of Marketing Qualifying Certificate Part 1, day-release and evenings; Institute of Marketing Qualifying Certificate Part 2; Institute of Marketing Dip in Marketing, evenings

Nene C, Northampton: Institute of Marketing Qualifying Certificate Part 1, evenings; Institute of Marketing Qualifying Certificate Part 2; Institute of Marketing Dip in Marketing, evenings

New C, Durham: Institute of Marketing Qualifying Certificate Part 1, evenings; Institute of Marketing Qualifying Certificate Part 2

Newcastle CAT: Institute of Marketing Qualifying Certificate Part 1, full-time and day-release; Institute of Marketing Qualifying Certificate Part 2

Newcastle Poly: Institute of Marketing Dip in Marketing, evenings; BTEC HND Business Studies, marketing specialism, full-time

Newry TC: Institute of Marketing Qualifying Certificate Part 1, evenings; Institute of Marketing Qualifying Certificate Part 2

North Cheshire C: Institute of Marketing Qualifying Certificate Part 2, day-release and evenings; Institute of Marketing Qualifying Certificate Part 2

North East London Poly: Institute of Marketing Dip in Marketing, day-release and evenings; Market Research Society Dip in Market Research, evenings

North East Wales IHE: BTEC HND Business Studies, marketing specialism, day-release

North Hertfordshire C: BTEC HND Business Studies, marketing specialism, full-time

North Worcestershire C: Institute of Marketing Qualifying Certificate Part 1, evenings; Institute of Marketing Qualifying Certificate Part 2; Institute of Marketing Dip in Marketing, evenings; BTEC HND Business Studies, marketing specialism, full-time

Park Lane CFE, Leeds: Institute of Marketing Qualifying Certificate Part 1, evenings; Institute of Marketing Qualifying Certificate Part 2

Plymouth CFE: Institute of Marketing Qualifying Certificate Part 1, day-release; Institute of Marketing Qualifying Certificate Part 2

Plymouth Poly: BTEC HND Business Studies, marketing specialism, full-time

Portsmouth Poly: BTEC HND Business Studies, marketing specialism, sandwich

Richmond CFE, Sheffield: Institute of Marketing Qualifying Certificate Part 1, full-time, day-release and evenings; Institute of Marketing Qualifying Certificate Part 2

Richmond-upon-Thames C: BTEC HND Business Studies, marketing specialism, full-time

St Helens CT: Institute of Marketing Qualifying Certificate Part 1, day-release; Institute of Marketing Qualifying Certificate Part 2; Institute of Marketing Dip in Marketing, day-release

St John's CFE, Manchester: Institute of Marketing Qualifying Certificate Part 1, evenings; Institute of Marketing Qualifying Certificate Part 2

Salford CT: Institute of Marketing Qualifying Certificate Part 1, day-release and evenings; Institute of Marketing Qualifying Certificate Part 2; Institute of Marketing Dip in Marketing, day-release and evenings; BTEC HND Business Studies, marketing specialism, full-time

Sheffield City Poly: Institute of Marketing Dip in Marketing, evenings

Slough CHE: Institute of Marketing Qualifying Certificate Part 1, day-release and evenings; Institute of Marketing Qualifying Certificate Part 2; Institute of Marketing Dip in Marketing, day-release and evenings

Southampton CHE: Institute of Marketing Dip in Marketing, day-release

South Bank Poly, London: Institute of Marketing Dip in Marketing, evenings

South Cheshire C: Institute of Marketing Qualifying Certificate Part 1, day-release and evenings; Institute of Marketing Qualifying Certificate Part 2

South Glamorgan IHE: Institute of Marketing Qualifying Certificate Part 1, evenings; Institute of Marketing Qualifying Certificate Part 2

South West London: Institute of Marketing Dip in Marketing, day-release and evenings

Staffordshire Poly: Institute of Marketing Dip in Marketing, day-release and evenings; BTEC HND Business Studies, marketing specialism, sandwich

Stockport CT: Institute of Marketing Qualifying Certificate Part 1, evenings; Institute of Marketing Qualifying Certificate Part 2; BTEC HND Business Studies, market research specialism, full-time and sandwich; BTEC HND Business Studies, marketing specialism, full-time and sandwich

Stoke Cauldon CFE: Institute of Marketing Qualifying Certificate Part 1, evenings; Institute of Marketing Qualifying Certificate Part 2; Institute of Marketing Dip in Marketing, evenings

Suffolk CH & FE: Institute of Marketing Qualifying Certificate Part 1, evenings; Institute of Marketing Qualifying Certificate Part 2; Institute of Marketing Dip in Marketing, day-release and evenings

Sutton Coldfield CFE: Institute of Marketing Qualifying Certificate Part 1, evenings; Institute of Marketing Qualifying Certificate Part 2

Teesside Poly: Institute of Marketing Dip in Marketing, day-release and evenings; BTEC HND Business Studies, marketing specialism, full-time

Thames Poly: BTEC HND Business Studies, marketing specialism, sandwich

Thurrock TC: Institute of Marketing Qualifying Certificate Part 1, evenings; Institute of Marketing Qualifying Certificate Part 2; RSA Commerce (Marketing) Stage 3, evenings

Tile Hill CFE, Coventry: Institute of Marketing Qualifying Certificate Part 1, evenings; Institute of Marketing Qualifying Certificate Part 2

Trent Poly: Institute of Marketing Qualifying Certificate Part 1, evenings; Institute of Marketing Qualifying Certificate Part 2; Institute of Marketing Dip in Marketing, evenings

Wales Poly: BTEC HND Business Studies, marketing specialism, sandwich
Watford College: Institute of Marketing Qualifying Certificate Part 1, evenings; Institute of Marketing Qualifying Certificate Part 2; Institute of Marketing Dip in Marketing, evenings; BTEC HND Business Studies, marketing specialism, full-time
West Bromwich CCT: Institute of Marketing Qualifying Certificate Part 1, full-time and evenings; Institute of Marketing Qualifying Certificate Part 2; Institute of Marketing Dip in Marketing, full-time, day-release and evenings
West Cumbria: Institute of Marketing Dip in Marketing, day-release
West Glamorgan IHE: BTEC HND Business Studies, marketing specialism, full-time
Wolverhampton Poly: Institute of Marketing Qualifying Certificate Part 1, day-release and evenings: Institute of Marketing Qualifying Certificate Part 2; Institute of Marketing Dip in Marketing, evenings
York CAT: Institute of Marketing Qualifying Certificate Part 1, evenings; Institute of Marketing Qualifying Certificate Part 2

Degrees of the Council for National Academic Awards

Courses in Hotel and Catering Management
Dorset, Poole: BSc Catering Administration
Huddersfield Poly: BSc (Hons) Catering Sciences and Applied Nutrition; BA Hotel and Catering Administration
Leeds Poly: BA Food and Accommodation Studies
Manchester Poly, Hollings Faculty: BSc Hotel and Catering Studies
Middlesex Poly: BSc Hotel and Catering Administration
Napier C, Edinburgh: BA Catering and Accommodation Studies
North London Poly: BSc Institutional Management
Oxford Poly: (Modular course – BA/BSc/BA(Hons)/ BSc (Hons)) Catering (double or single field); Food and Nutrition (single field); DipHE
Portsmouth Poly: BA Hotel and Catering Management
Robert Gordon's Institute of Technology, Aberdeen: BA Hotel, Catering and Institutional Administration
Sheffield Poly: BSc (Hons) Catering Systems
Ulster Poly, Newtownabbey: BA Hons, Catering Administration

Courses in Public Relations
Central London Poly: BA (Hons) Media Studies, full-time
Coventry Poly: BA (Hons) Communication Studies, full-time
Glasgow: BA Communication Studies, full-time
Manchester Poly: BA (Hons) Design for Communication Media, full-time
Queen Margaret C, Edinburgh: BA Communication Studies, full-time

Sheffield City Poly: BA/BA (Hons) Communication Studies, full-time
Sunderland Poly: BA/BA (Hons) Communication Studies, full-time
Trent Poly: BA (Hons) Communication Studies, full-time
Ulster Poly: BSc (Hons) Human Communication, full-time
Wales Poly: BA (Hons) Communication Studies, full-time

Courses in Marketing
Bristol Poly: Dip in Marketing, full-time
Thames Poly: BA (Hons) International Marketing, sandwich
Sheffield Poly: BSc (Hons) Food Marketing Science

University Degree Courses

Degrees in Hotel and Catering
University C, Cardiff: BSc (Hons) Hotel and Institutional Management
Dorset IHE: BA (Hons) Hospitality Management
Ealing CHE: BA and BA (Hons) Catering and Tourism Management
Strathclyde University, Glasgow: BA/BA (Hons) Hotel and Catering Management
Surrey University, Guildford: BSc (Hons) Hotel and Catering Administration; BSc Hotel Management

Degrees in Public Relations
Bristol Poly: Combined Subjects Degree, Communication Studies option
Dorset IHE: BA/BA (Hons) English and Media Studies, full-time (Awarded by Southampton University)
Goldsmiths' C, London: Combined Subjects Degree, Communication Studies option; full-time
Normal College of Education, Bangor: BA Communications, full-time (Awarded by University of Wales); Combined Subjects Degree, Communication Studies option, full-time
North Cheshire C: BA Media and Communication, full-time (Awarded by Manchester University)
Trinity and All Saints C, Leeds: BA/BA (Hons)/BSc/BSc (Hons) Public Media and another subject, full-time (Awarded by Leeds University); Combined Subjects Degree, Communication Arts and Media option, full-time

Degrees in Marketing
City of London Poly: Combined Subjects Degree with marketing option, full-time and day-release; Business Studies Degree, marketing option, sandwich
Leicester Poly: Business Studies Degree, marketing option, full-time

North Staffordshire Poly: Business Studies Degree, marketing option, sandwich
Teesside Poly: Business Studies Degree, marketing option, sandwich

Degrees in Tourism
Dorset IHE: CNAA BA (Hons) Tourism Studies, 4 year sandwich
New C, Durham: CNAA BA (Hons) Travel & Tourism, 4 years full-time
Newcastle Poly: CNAA BA (Hons) Travel & Tourism, 4 years sandwich
Oxford Poly: Combined subjects degree with tourism option, 3 years full-time or 5 part-time
South Glamorgan IHE: CNAA BA Travel & Tourism, 4 years sandwich

Postgraduate Degrees in Tourism
University of Birmingham: Dip in Tourism and Leisure Services
Manchester Polytechnic, Hollings Faculty: Postgraduate Dip in Travel/Tourism, one year
Strathclyde University, Glasgow: MSc Tourism; Postgraduate Dip in Tourism
Surrey University, Guildford: MSc Tourism Planning and Development; MSc Tourism Marketing; MSc Tourism Studies; Postgraduate course in Tourism, one year

ABTA-Approved Training Centres for YTS Courses

Dundee College of Commerce
Harlow Technical College
Henley College of Further Education, Coventry
Lancaster and Morecambe College of Further Education
Lewes Technical College
Loughborough Technical College
Mid Cornwall College of Further Education, St Austell
New College, Durham
Norwich City College
Paddington College, London
Park Lane College of Further Education, Leeds
St Helens College of Technology
Shrewsbury Technical College
South Glamorgan Institute of Higher Education, Cardiff
Southport Technical College
South Trafford College of Further Education
South Warwickshire College of Further Education
Southwark College, London SE1
Stockport College of Technology
Tresham College, Kettering
York College of Arts & Technology

Chapter 11
Useful Addresses

ABTA National Training Board, Barratt House, 11 Chertsey Road, Woking, Surrey GU21 5AL; 04862 27321

Association of Graduate Careers Advisory Services, Central Services Unit, Crawford House, Precinct Centre, Oxford Road, Manchester M13 9EP; 061-273 4233

Business and Technician Education Council, Central House, Upper Woburn Place, London WC1H OHH; 01-388 3288

Careers & Occupational Information Centre, Moorfoot, Sheffield S1 4PQ; 0742 753275

Chartered Institute of Transport, 80 Portland Place, London W1N 4DP; 01-580 5216

City and Guilds of London Institute, 76 Portland Place, London W1N 4AA; 01-580 3050

Countryside Commission, Publications Despatch Department, 19 Albert Road, Manchester M19 2EQ; 061-224 6287

English Tourist Board, 24 Grosvenor Gardens, London SW1; 01-730 3450

Hotel and Catering Training Board, International House, High Street, Ealing, London W5 5DB; 01-579 2400

Hotel Catering and Institutional Management Association, 191 Trinity Road, London SW17 7HN; 01-672 4251

Institute of Leisure and Amenity Management, Lower Basildon, Reading, Berkshire RG8 9NE; 0491 873558

Institute of Travel and Tourism, 113 Victoria Street, St Albans, Hertfordshire AL1 3TJ; 0727 54395

Museums Association, 34 Bloomsbury Way, London WC1A 2SF; 01-404 4764

The Tourism Society (for publications), 26 Grosvenor Gardens, London SW1

Scottish Vocational Education Council, 24 Douglas Street, Glasgow G2 7NG; 041-248 7900

Regional Advisory Councils

For information about courses, you could approach the Regional Advisory Council for Further Education:

East Anglia: 2 Looms Lane, Bury St Edmunds, Suffolk IHE 2AN; 0284 64977

East Midlands: Robins Wood House, Robins Wood Road, Aspley, Nottingham NG8 3NH; 0602 293291

London and Home Counties: Tavistock House South, Tavistock Square, London WC1H 9LR; 01-388 0027

North: 5 Grosvenor Villas, Grosvenor Road, Newcastle upon Tyne NE2 2RU; 091-281 3242

North West: The Town Hall, Walkden Road, Worsley, Manchester M28 4QE; 061-702 8700

South: 26 Bath Road, Reading RG1 6NT; 0734 52120

South West: Wessex Lodge, 11-13 Billetfield, Taunton, Somerset TA1 3NN; 0823 85491

Wales: 245 Western Avenue, Cardiff CF5 2YX; 0222 561231

West Midlands: Norfolk House, Smallbrook Queensway, Birmingham B5 4NB; 021-643 8924

Yorkshire and Humberside: Bowling Green Terrace, Jack Lane, Leeds LS11 9SX; 0532 440751

Chapter 12
Useful Publications

Britmark (incorporating *Tourism Society Yearbook*, which contains information on education and training in tourism, including list of colleges with tourism courses). Tourism Society
Careers in Hotel and Catering Management, 3rd edition, Kogan Page
A Handbook of Careers in Tourism and Leisure, Hobsons
Jobs in Airports, Kogan Page
Jobs in Hotels, 2nd edition, Kogan Page
Jobs in Travel and Tourism, Kogan Page
Skills for Tourism, COIC
Working in Airports, COIC
Working in Tourism, COIC

Useful Journals

The following journals advertise job vacancies for the travel and holiday industry:

Campaign
Caterer & Hotelkeeper
Travel News
Travel Trade Gazette